Iowa

Iowa

Martin Hintz

Children's Press®
A Division of Grolier Publishing
New York   London   Hong Kong   Sydney
Danbury, Connecticut

Frontispiece: The Upper Iowa River

Front cover: A farm in Eldorado

Back cover: State capitol

Consultant: Linda Wessell, Education Coordinator, State Historical Society of Iowa

Please note: All statistics are as up-to-date as possible at the time of publication.

Visit Children's Press on the Internet at http://publishing.grolier.com

Book production by Editorial Directions, Inc.

Library of Congress Cataloging-in-Publication Data

Hintz, Martin.
    Iowa / Martin Hintz.
      p. cm. — (America the beautiful. Second series)
    Includes bibliographical references and index.
    Summary : Describes the geography, history, economy, culture, and people of the
state of Iowa.
    ISBN 0-516-21070-X
    1. Iowa Juvenile literature. [1. Iowa.] I. Title. II. Series.
F621.3.H56 2000   99-25688
979.5—dc21   CIP
                                                                   AC

Acknowledgments

The author wishes to thank the many Iowans who helped him with this book. The assistance provided by governmental and tourism officials, especially Jana DeBrower, executive director of the Eastern Iowa Tourism Association, was greatly appreciated. Special nods also go to Gertrude Hintz, Harold and Wilma Hintz, Albert and Gertrude Russell, all the other Russells, the Larsons, Howie and Mary Therese Wemark and their family, Jeanne Cissne, the Armstrongs, the Howards, the Wronkas, Tom and Sue Barnes, Richard and Margie Natvig, Eileen Kennedy and her clan, the nuns at St. Joseph's grade school, the teachers at New Hampton Community High School, Vera Bradshaw, Minnette Doderer, Harold Hughes, the guys on the road crew, the neighbors back home, and dozens of others who were always proud of being Iowans.

Iowa farm

Cedar Rapids

Cornfields

Contents

Ring-necked pheasant

The town of Elkader

Winter in Iowa

Iowans

Folk musicians

CHAPTER ONE

Hello, Iowa

Iowa farmers talking

Iowa is a people-friendly place where folks you don't know often say hello. Drivers of the giant grain trucks on U.S. Highway 18 have a greeting they call the Iowa Salute. Holding onto the steering wheel of their big rigs, they'll smile and raise an index finger in greeting as they pass. In Iowa, manners are important and people look after one another.

Roadways all over the state lead to wonderful scenic discoveries. In the fertile hillsides and prairie lands of western Iowa, the Loess Hills Scenic Byway follows the Missouri River. On the other side of the state, the Great River Road meanders along the Mississippi River, with its rugged limestone bluffs and prehistoric burial sites.

In the south, the Mormon Pioneer Trail tracks the rugged, winding route that thousands of pioneers from the Church of Jesus Christ of Latter-day Saints followed. Fleeing religious persecution in the East, they sought a new life near the Great Salt Lake in Utah.

Opposite: A full moon over an Iowa farm

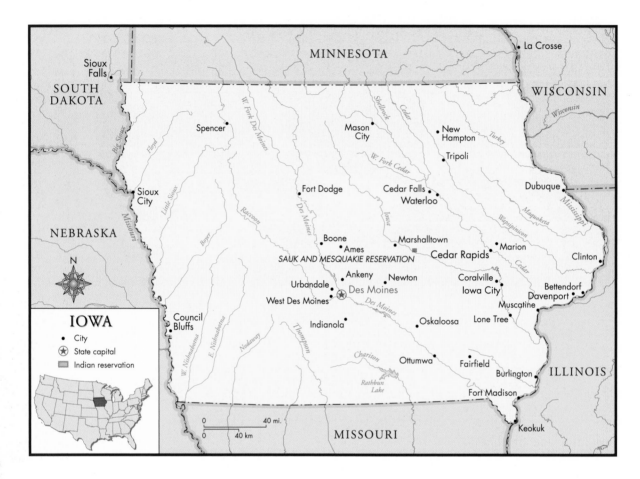

MINNESOTA

La Crosse

Sioux Falls

SOUTH DAKOTA

WISCONSIN

Spencer

Mason City

New Hampton

Tripoli

Dubuque

Sioux City

Fort Dodge

Cedar Falls
Waterloo

NEBRASKA

Boone
Ames

Marshalltown

Marion

Clinton

SAUK AND MESQUAKIE RESERVATION

Cedar Rapids

Urbandale

Ankeny

Newton

Coralville

Des Moines

Iowa City

Bettendorf
Davenport

West Des Moines

Muscatine

IOWA

• City
⭐ State capital
▪ Indian reservation

Council Bluffs

Indianola

Oskaloosa

Lone Tree

Ottumwa

Fairfield

Burlington

ILLINOIS

Rathbun Lake

Fort Madison

0 ___ 40 mi.
0 ___ 40 km

MISSOURI

Keokuk

Geopolitical map of Iowa

The 200-mile (322-kilometer) Dragoon Trail is named after the lightly armed cavalry soldiers who scouted the Iowa frontier in the 1830s and established outposts from Des Moines to Fort Dodge.

The Lewis and Clark Trail traces Meriwether Lewis and William Clark's journey along the Missouri River. At the beginning of the 1800s, these two explorers were sent by President Thomas Jefferson to map the land acquired in the Louisiana Purchase.

Grant Wood, a famous American painter, is memorialized by a scenic byway in central Iowa named in his honor. Traveling along

Opposite: The state is known for its wide-open spaces.

Iowa winters bring lots of snow.

the route helps explain how the state's beautiful vistas inspired the artist.

In the northeastern part of the state is the River Bluffs Scenic Byway, a roller-coaster ride through farm country. Southeastern Iowa has the Woodlands Scenic Byway, which takes motorists through dense hardwood forests. The Iowa River Valley Scenic Byway follows the state's namesake river as it moves through the heart of Iowa. On the far western edge of the state, the Western Skies Scenic Byway offers even more wide-open places and historic villages just off Interstate 80.

Although Iowa has its urban scene of theaters, nightclubs, museums, concert halls, and factories, the pull of the open land—in winter, spring, summer, and fall—is all-powerful. Even amid the growing urban sprawl, with its fast-food restaurants and shopping malls, an Iowan is never far from fields, pastures, streams, and woodlands.

CHAPTER TWO

Exploring the Prairie Land

Flying over eastern Iowa's Mississippi River bluffs, you might see what appear to be birds and bears marching across the landscape. These mounds of earth shaped like animals were built between 500 B.C. and A.D. 1300. They may have been the territorial markers or religious sites of prehistoric Indian people known as the Mound Builders. Dozens of these remarkable figures, or effigies, are preserved at the Effigy Mounds National Monument, northwest of Marquette. Park rangers continue to find unmapped mounds in the forests near the Mississippi.

Indian mounds at the Effigy Mounds National Monument

The Mound Builders were members of ancient Adena, Mississippian, and Hopewell cultures. Their distant relatives lived throughout the Mississippi River Valley. These settled groups farmed grain such as corn and hunted animals. Their stone tools and pieces of pottery tell a fascinating story, but they faded into history well before the ancestors of today's Native American people arrived in the area. The early Mound Builders lived in these prairies and hills for thousands of years before the arrival of the first Europeans.

In the 1600s, about twenty different tribes lived in what is now Iowa. Among them were the Ioway, Sauk, Mesquakie (sometimes called the Fox), Oto, and Missouri. The Sioux regularly hunted in northern Iowa from their main bases in Minnesota and the Dakotas.

Opposite: The Old Zion Church in Burlington was Iowa's first territorial capitol.

Eventually, the Sauk and Mesquakie became the most powerful tribes in the Upper Mississippi River Valley. They had moved from Michigan into Wisconsin and western Illinois and eastern Iowa by the 1730s. They lived in villages only in winter. At the first sign of spring, they packed up their gear and moved north into Minnesota to tap maple trees for sap. In summer, they traveled around their extensive hunting grounds.

Louis Jolliet and Father Jacques Marquette on the Mississippi River

Iowa's First Europeans

In the summer of 1673, French explorer Louis Jolliet and Father Jacques Marquette, a French Jesuit priest, canoed down the Wisconsin River into the Mississippi River. On June 25, they landed on the Iowa side of the wide Mississippi. In their journals, the two men recorded that the western riverbank was lush and fertile.

In 1680, explorer René-Robert Cavelier, Sieur de La Salle, sent one of his men, Michael Aco, and Father Louis Hennepin to explore the Upper Mississippi while he traveled on to the mouth of the river. On their way, Aco and Hennepin remarked on Iowa's natural beauty. In 1682, La Salle claimed all the land drained by the Mississippi, including Iowa, for King Louis XIV of France. He named the entire area *Louisiana*.

Over the next half-century, only a few missionaries and fur traders ventured down the Mississippi River toward Iowa. In 1690, Nicholas Perrot taught Miami Indians how to mine lead near what is now Dubuque, but it was years before Europeans settled there permanently.

In 1788, the Mesquakie Indians allowed Julien Dubuque, a French Canadian, to mine lead near where Perrot had found the rich mineral. Because the territory was Spanish—France gave up its claim to the land in 1762—Dubuque needed approval from the Spaniards. They eventually awarded Dubuque a land grant in 1796, and he lived in the area until his death in 1810. Dubuque is considered Iowa's first European settler.

Julien Dubuque

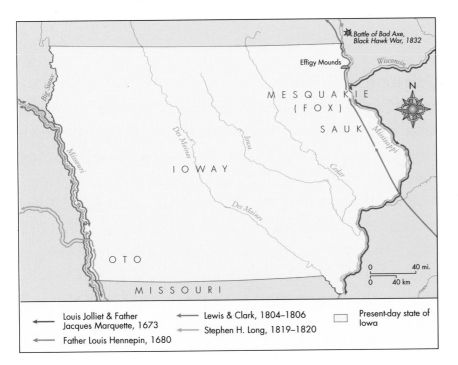

Exploration of Iowa

The Louisiana Purchase

Spain returned the territory west of the Mississippi River to France in 1800. Then, in 1803, France sold it to the United States in a deal called the Louisiana Purchase. President Thomas Jefferson sent Meriwether Lewis and William Clark to explore the new territory in 1804. They crossed Iowa and headed into the vast Great Plains, returning in 1806.

In an effort to govern this huge region, the United States divided the Louisiana Purchase land into the territory of Orleans and the district of Louisiana, which included Iowa. At first, Iowa was administered by the governor of Indiana Territory, however. Iowa was included in a revamped region called Louisiana Territory in 1805. In 1812, it became part of Missouri Territory. When Missouri became a state in 1821, Iowa had no government for several years.

Other Explorers

In 1805, army officer Zebulon M. Pike traveled the Mississippi River looking for good sites on which to build forts. He paid a social call at Dubuque's outpost and saw the potential for mining more lead.

It wasn't long before others came through the region. Explorers Henry R. Schoolcraft, Albert M. Lea, and Stephen H. Long were among those early visitors whose work helped open up much of the Upper Mississippi River Valley to settlement by white people. As more whites came, the original Native American inhabitants of Iowa grew worried.

The Black Hawk War

During this period, the interior of Iowa was closed to settlement, and only Native Americans lived there. But trouble loomed for the Indians.

In 1829, the U.S. government ordered the Sauk and the Mesquakie to leave Illinois and Wisconsin and move permanently to Iowa. Although the federal government claimed Illinois under a treaty dating back to 1804, Sauk chief Black Hawk objected and returned to Illinois to harvest corn in 1832. Black Hawk said that the treaty—which gave the Indians only a few barrels of whiskey and gunpowder and some cash in exchange for their land—was unfair.

When Black Hawk and his people appeared in Illinois, the white settlers panicked. Troops were called to chase out the Indians. Over the next three months, Black Hawk led 400 Sauk north into Wisconsin. When they tried to surrender in western Wisconsin, where the Bad Axe River flows into the Mississippi, they were driven into the water. Troops aboard an army gunboat shot and killed many of the women, children, and old people trying to swim to safety. Most of those who made it to the Iowa shore were then massacred by a

Chief Black Hawk

The Battle of Bad Axe

Sioux war party waiting for them. This deadly affair was called the Black Hawk War.

As punishment for fighting, the Sauk and Mesquakie were forced to give up a strip of land 50 miles (80 km) wide. This land, known as the Black Hawk Purchase, stretched along the Mississippi River from the Missouri border to northeastern Iowa. Many settlers moved in.

Newcomers

When the fear of Indian unrest had passed, whites quickly populated the land. Newcomers from such states as Kentucky, Tennessee, Virginia, New York, Indiana, Illinois, Missouri, Ohio, and Pennsylvania flooded the area, eager to farm the rich soil.

A Young President in Battle

Abraham Lincoln was a young Illinois militiaman during the Black Hawk War. He was awarded two farms near Garwin and Denison in Iowa for his service during the conflict. ■

Some homes in early Iowa were made of sod.

Iowa's pioneers found the midwestern land different from the heavily wooded east. Iowa was mostly tallgrass prairies. Some newcomers had a hard time finding enough wood to build a house, so they turned to a readily available substitute—sod. Thick blocks of soil were cut and stacked to make walls sturdy enough to hold a roof. These well-insulated earthen homes were warm in winter and cool in summer.

From Territory to Statehood

The U.S. Congress, realizing that somebody had to administer the region, attached Iowa to Michigan Territory in 1834. Two years later, Michigan became a state and Iowa was attached to Wisconsin Territory. Finally in 1838, Iowa Territory, which included large chunks of Minnesota and the Dakotas, was established.

Robert Lucas, the former Democratic governor of Ohio, was

Robert Lucas, Iowa's first territorial governor

named the first territorial governor. A territorial capital was established at Burlington and then moved to Iowa City in 1841. Lucas began working toward making Iowa a state shortly after taking office but, being cautious, Iowans were slow to pick up on the idea. As long as Iowa remained a territory, the federal government would pay governing officials' salaries, but if Iowa became a state, taxes would have to be raised to pay the bureaucrats. And nobody wanted to pay more taxes. However, Lucas and his successors, John Chambers and James Clarke, were patient and persistent.

By 1844, Iowans were finally convinced they would fare better economically as a state and met to draft a constitution. A disagreement with Congress over the proposed state boundaries

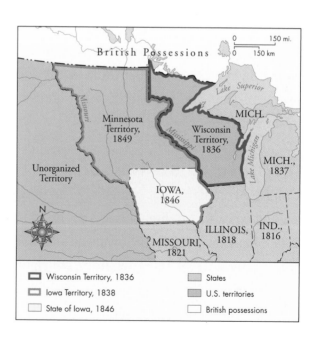

Historical map of Iowa

followed. Originally, the delegates wanted Iowa to extend as far north as St. Paul, Minnesota, but Congress proposed a much smaller region—about half as much land. Iowa voters rejected that proposal in 1845.

Over the next few months, a compromise was hammered out, and in 1846, a second constitutional convention was held at the territorial capital in Iowa City. After agreeing on Iowa's boundaries, the convention delegates approved a document and Congress gave its approval. On December 28, 1846, President James K. Polk officially declared Iowa the twenty-ninth state. Democrat Ansel Briggs was Iowa's first governor.

President James K. Polk was in office when Iowa became a state in 1846.

Steps Toward Statehood

1803	Louisiana Purchase includes Iowa.
1805	Iowa becomes part of Louisiana Territory.
1812	Missouri Territory created, which includes Iowa.
1821	Iowa becomes unorganized land after state of Missouri is created.
1834	Iowa attached to Michigan Territory.
1836	Iowa attached to Wisconsin Territory.
1838	Iowa Territory established on July 4.
1839	Territorial Governor Robert Lucas encourages statehood.
1844	First constitutional convention called but constitution is rejected by voters.
1846	Iowa voters approve second state constitution on August 3. Iowa becomes a state on December 28.

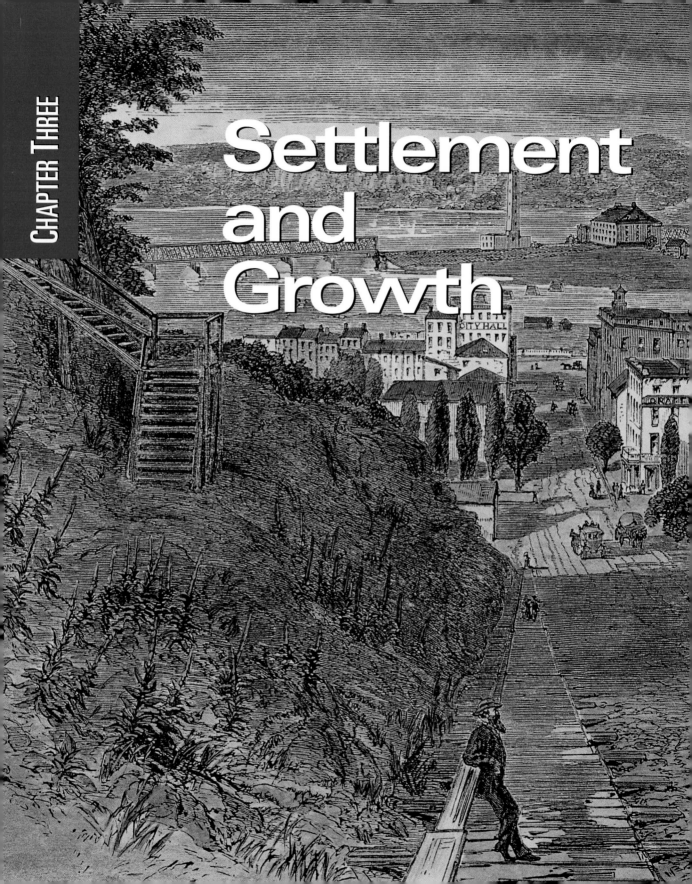

CHAPTER THREE

Settlement and Growth

After Iowa became a state, thousands of pioneers poured across the Mississippi River, attracted by the cheap land and wide-open space. Many felt crowded on their small farms back east. Others wanted to escape the big-city slums. Some were just looking for adventure.

It wasn't an easy life. From dawn to dusk, entire families cleared land, broke sod, fed and watered livestock, and planted and harvested crops.

Settlers also faced locusts, windstorms, drought, and floods. Prairie fires often swept over the landscape, forcing men, women, and children to beat the flames away from their fields. The danger did not end until the first snow fell.

Natural disasters were not the only challenges that the settlers faced. Accidents were an everyday occurrence on pioneer homesteads. And deadly diseases such as scarlet fever and smallpox often struck towns and farming communities, killing young and old. Many babies died soon after birth because there were very few doctors and no hospitals.

Notices such as this one lured many settlers to Iowa and other states.

Spirit Lake

The harsh winter of 1857 affected both the settlers and the few remaining Native Americans living in the far northwestern part of Iowa, setting the stage for a tragic incident. In March, a band of

Opposite: Dubuque in the nineteenth century

Settlers coped with brushfires and other natural disasters.

starving Sioux men, women, and children, angry at the growing number of whites in the area, attacked settlers' cabins near Spirit Lake.

During the fighting, more than thirty settlers were killed and four women were kidnapped. Two eventually died in captivity and the two others were released with the help of sympathetic Indians. After this conflict, Iowa was spared any more such incidents. In 1895, Iowa set up a memorial in Spirit Lake for those who had died.

In spite of the ever-present dangers, never-ending chores, and rugged living conditions, people continued to come to Iowa. The rewards of the land were great and most settlers stayed.

Civil War

While pioneers settled Iowa, the nation was breaking apart over slavery, states' rights, and economics. Iowa was a free state where slavery was outlawed and most residents opposed treating other human beings as property.

The slavery issue became a rallying point for many Iowans when the Civil War eventually broke out in 1861. Although no

General Grenville Dodge played a key role in the Union army during the Civil War.

battles were fought on its soil, the state sent more than 75,000 men to the Union army. Of that number, some 12,000 soldiers died in the fighting or perished from disease in the crowded, dirty camps and hospitals.

During the war, Iowans distinguished themselves in many ways. One notable soldier from Iowa was General Grenville Dodge, who rebuilt many damaged railroads in occupied Southern states. He also directed counterintelligence activities for the Union army, rooting out Southern sympathizers who relayed information on troop movements to the Confederacy.

Iowa women did their part to help in the war effort. They served as nurses, formed soldier-relief societies, sewed uniforms, and made bandages. After a visit to one Union hospital to see her wounded brother, Annie Wittenmyer complained that greasy bacon and cold coffee was not good enough for the injured soldiers. She

Annie Wittenmyer worked to improve Civil War hospitals.

demanded that military hospitals establish kitchens to prepare healthy meals, and many of them did. After the war, Wittenmyer founded several homes for soldiers' orphans.

Right to Vote for Women

With peace, Iowa's political scene changed. Democrats had traditionally been the state's strongest party. But from the mid-1850s, the new Republican Party grew stronger and dominated until 1932. The issue of giving women the vote, however, crossed party lines.

In 1870, both houses of the Iowa General Assembly passed a suffrage amendment. But before it went to the public for a vote, support died. For the next forty-seven years, women continued to fight for their right to vote. Their day finally came in 1920, when the Nineteenth Amendment to the U.S. Constitution was passed.

Railroads and Economic Growth

The first settlers had to ship most of their goods on steamboats down the Mississippi River to New Orleans on the Gulf of Mexico. The trip took as long as two weeks, and produce often spoiled. By the late 1850s, more than a dozen rail lines served Chicago, and Iowans looked at the city as an example. The state knew it had to set up railroad service quickly if it hoped to compete. In 1867,

Council Bluffs became a major stop for the Union Pacific Railroad, completing the final link in the first U.S. transcontinental railway. Within a decade after the end of the Civil War, five railroad lines crossed the state.

Trains changed the face of Iowa. By the end of the 1900s, at least six trains stopped each day at even the smallest villages on the railway lines. The trains brought new people to town, hauled goods, carried freight and mail, and served as a link to the rest of the country.

The railroads also helped increase the state's income. Corn, pork, and beef shipped to Chicago's markets brought good prices. Shipping agricultural products was easier, cheaper, and quicker by train than by wagon or steamboat. Access to bigger markets helped John and Robert Stuart and their cousin George Douglas start

In 1867, the first Union Pacific train traveled from Connecticut to Iowa with 360 passengers.

A Musical College

In 1861, Norwegian Lutherans founded Luther College in Decorah, Iowa. The college has always been strong in the field of music. Its concert band, started in 1876, quickly gained a national reputation and toured Europe in 1914. Luther College's symphony orchestra has traveled abroad a great deal, performing six times in Vienna, Austria. ■

Quaker Oats in the late 1800s. It is now one of the world's largest cereal-processing companies. Meatpacking was also a major industry by the 1870s. Cedar Rapids' Sinclair Meat Packing and Ottumwa's John Morrell and Company fed the East Coast's exploding population with tons of their potted meat.

Iowa Wesleyan College was founded in 1842.

The Importance of Education

From Iowa's pioneer beginnings, schools were always among the first buildings in a community. The state's first grade school opened in 1830, with Berryman Jennings as its only teacher. Iowa Wesleyan College, one of the oldest colleges in Iowa, was established in 1842 in Mount Pleasant.

Within a few years, Catholics and Methodists founded five more colleges in Iowa.

Iowa's Grinnell College, founded in 1847 by Congregationalist ministers, led the country with many educational firsts. In 1871, Hannibal Kershaw from Grinnell became the first African-American graduate from a college west of the Mississippi River. Besides being one of the first colleges in the United States to enroll women on an equal basis, Grinnell also instituted the nation's first political science department.

World Events

Although Iowa is in the center of the United States, it has been greatly affected by world events. In 1898, the state sent four infantry regiments to fight in the Spanish-American War. Another unit served in the Philippines at the turn of the century. After the United States entered World War I in 1917, more than 113,000 Iowans joined the military, and 2,000 lost their lives. On the home front, the farm community produced extra food for the troops. The resulting prosperity allowed farmers to buy more land and raise more pork and beef and grow more corn.

But the boom times did not last long. When the war ended, some farmers had overextended themselves and were in deep debt. Then farm prices hit an all-time low. By the 1920s, many farmers had trouble paying off what they owed. The worldwide economic collapse of the Great Depression hit them hard. Banks closed, businesses shut down, and many workers lost their jobs and their homes.

President Herbert Hoover was born in Iowa.

Iowa-born president Herbert Hoover did what he could for all Americans when he took office in 1929, but the challenges were great. Hoover's philosophy of letting the markets dictate policies did not work well when the crumbling financial world affected everyone. Farmers tried to survive without any governmental support. Some joined the Farm Holiday Association, which tried to withhold products from the market in an effort to raise prices. Sometimes violence flared on the blockade lines; milk trucks were tipped over and livestock trucks were hijacked.

Franklin D. Roosevelt, who became president in 1933, took a more active role to help farmers. The president asked Henry A. Wallace, an Iowan born to a farm family, to serve as secretary of agriculture. Wallace was elected vice president in 1940. He was later made secretary of commerce, a position he held until 1946.

World War II

When the United States entered World War II in 1941, Iowa again rallied around the flag. About 286,000 Iowans served in the armed forces. Of that number, some 6,000 died. Navy fliers trained in Ottumwa and Iowa City. Giant munitions plants at Ankeny and

A student army training corps at the University of Iowa during World War II

Burlington churned out millions of bullets and tons of bombs by the end of the war in 1945.

On the home front, farm families worked long hours to grow and harvest food for hungry troops. Kids planted Victory Gardens to keep fresh vegetables on the dinner table, and women contributed to the war effort as they had in the past. The country's first Women's Army Corps training camp was located at Fort Des Moines.

CHAPTER FOUR

Booms and Bad Times

Many Iowans found factory work after World War II.

Along with the rest of the United States, Iowa enjoyed an economic boom during the 1950s. Men and women returning home from the military reentered the workforce or went to college, helped by low-interest government loans under the GI Bill. They made Iowa one of the most productive states in the Midwest within a few years. Some veterans had to go to war again in Korea in the early 1950s. Of 85,314 Iowans who served in the military during that bloody conflict, 532 died.

Despite the relative peace at home, there were always challenges. One controversial issue of the day involved liquor sales. In Iowa, people could buy alcohol only at state-run liquor stores, where taxes kept prices high. For years, taverns could not sell hard liquor, only low-alcohol beer. Many people traveled to neighboring states to purchase less expensive liquor and stronger beer. In 1963, after much debate, Iowans relaxed their restrictions on liquor sales.

A Changing Political System

In the postwar years, it became clear that Iowa needed a political system that represented its residents more fairly. Throughout

Opposite: The President Riverboat Casino near Davenport

Maharishi University

Maharishi University of Management was founded by Maharishi Mahesh Yogi in 1971. Students receive degrees in many traditional fields, but the school, located in Fairfield, emphasizes harmonious living. ■

most of the 1800s, seats in the legislature were drawn up on the basis of population, and one legislator usually represented about four counties. However, as the population grew, some counties had more voters than others. Residents in the more populous regions thought they should have a greater say in how the state was run. Rural areas objected to any changes, fearing they would lose political power.

In 1904, a constitutional amendment granted each county one legislator. Nine of the most populous counties got two representatives. In 1928, another amendment specified that no county would have more than one senator, though seats were supposed to be allocated according to population. There were no changes for the next thirty years.

In 1960, 53 percent of the population lived in urban areas, up from about 25 percent in 1900. Powerful conservatives joined forces with the Iowa Farm Bureau Federation and other rural interest groups to block any changes. They were concerned that less state money would be available for roads and other projects in rural areas. Labor groups, chambers of commerce, and organizations such as the League of Women Voters and the League of Municipalities opposed this view.

In the 1960s and 1970s, legislators suggested several plans for reapportionment—a redrawing of legislative district lines. Voters rejected a plan in 1963, but in 1964 the federal courts ordered the state to reapportion the districts. The 1965 legislature then modified a temporary plan that gave more representation to the cities and increased the number of senators. After the 1970 census, the state reapportioned the districts again. Iowa's supreme court declared the plan unconstitutional and put forth its own plan, which took effect in 1972.

After the 1980 census, the state was again reapportioned. These updates accommodated the shifting population mix in the state. The Iowa legislature now has one of the country's fairest systems for electing its representatives.

The Vietnam War and the 1960s

The 1960s was an emotional period in Iowa—and all America—as the generations argued over the direction of the country. In 1965, U.S. troops were sent to fight in the Vietnam War, which raged in Southeast Asia from 1957 to 1975.

Margaret Mullen wrote *Friendly Fire* after her son was killed in Vietnam.

As the war ground on, more and more Iowans questioned the government's decisions. Antiwar protests, marches, and sit-ins took place. Senator Harold Hughes, a Democrat from Iowa, became a national leader for peace. Margaret (Peg) Mullen, wife of a farmer from Black Hawk County, became an antiwar activist after misdirected American artillery fire killed her son. Her story, told in a book called *Friendly Fire*, was made into a television movie. The last U.S. troops left Vietnam in 1973. Civil rights and women's issues also stirred the state's social pot during this time.

A Natural Disaster

The Great Flood of 1993 was one of the worst natural disasters in Iowa's history. Rain and snow runoff raised the rivers and streams to dangerous levels. Because many wetlands had been lost to urban sprawl and farming, water from the Missouri, Mississippi, Des Moines, Cedar, and Iowa Rivers had no safe place to go. For weeks, there was media coverage of motorboats on main streets, stranded cattle, and submerged fields. The floods caused millions of dollars in damages; Des Moines had no water system for six weeks. Years after the disaster, some of the hardest-hit areas were still recovering. ■

Bad Times for Farmers

On the economic front, the state's farming boom went bust during the 1980s. Support for agricultural issues declined, prices plummeted, land values dipped, and international markets dried up. These factors jeopardized many small farming operations. In 1998,

only 280,000 Iowans still lived on about 100,000 family farms—
less than half the number of farms in the state fifty years earlier. As
small farmers struggle to compete with large corporations, many
mothers and fathers have had to take outside jobs to keep their
farms.

During the 1980s, many Iowa farms suffered.

In 1986, the Iowa General Assembly established a Farmer-Creditor Service and a Farmer Legal Assistance Program to help small farmers stay in business and on their property. Youth organizations such as Future Farmers of America and 4-H work hard to develop programs to keep young people interested in agriculture. Both organizations have expanded their projects to Iowa's cities.

The decline of small farms has affected Iowa's economy in more ways than one. For example, because farmers have cut back on new equipment, tractor sales have dropped, which has led to factory layoffs.

Raising hogs is one way to make a living in Iowa.

At the end of the 1990s, another agricultural issue was the growth of vast hog lots. As the corporate pig farmers explain, it is more cost-efficient to raise 10,000 hogs than 100 hogs. But the pollution associated with these operations make many Iowans wonder if larger is really better. Faced with competition and declining prices, some small Iowa farmers simply gave away their hogs in 1998. It cost more to raise the pigs than to sell them.

Iowa Adapts

Even with the changes in the agricultural world, all was not lost. The state adapted. Iowa businesses turned their corporate power toward improving their products. Pioneer Hi-Bred International developed numerous varieties of hybrid corn seed, with test sites from Canada to Zimbabwe.

By 1970, industry had overtaken agriculture as the state's primary source of income. Iowa factories make many products, from horse trailers in Cresco to windows for recreational vehicles in New Hampton. The rise of these small businesses kept the economy afloat. Des Moines and Cedar Rapids became business centers for banks, publishing operations, and insurance, computer, and telemarketing companies.

Lois H. Tiffany

Scientists helped Iowa adapt too. Among them was Lois H. Tiffany, nicknamed the Mushroom Lady because of her work in edible—and non-edible—fungi. A professor at Iowa State University, she still leaves her lab in Ames regularly to visit high schools and encourage students, particularly young women, to study math and the sciences. Tiffany was the first recipient of the Governor's Medal for Science Teaching.

An Important Visitor

On October 4, 1979, Pope John Paul II visited the Living History Farms, an agricultural museum in West Des Moines that features a fully operating 1850 pioneer farm. The pope came after receiving a letter from a farmer named Joe Hays, who attended Saint Patrick's Church in the small town of Cumming.

It took the museum forty-five days to carry out all the preparations—from sprucing up the grounds to trucking in more than 4,500 portable toilets for the 400,000 people who attended the mass. The pope gave the mass standing in front of a giant quilt— made by local farming women— that depicted the four seasons, with a cross in the center to represent the people's faith.

In 1999, the museum held a twentieth-anniversary commemoration of Pope John Paul II's visit. It was sponsored by the Roman Catholic Diocese of Des Moines. ∎

Growth of Minorities

As the economy grows, more and more minorities, including Thai, Vietnamese, and Hmong refugees, find Iowa a good place to live and work. For example, the small northeastern Iowa town of Postville is home to one of the country's largest processors of kosher turkey products and, as a result, the town has a growing population of Orthodox Jews. Additionally, Postville includes a wonderful mix of Norwegian Lutherans, Hispanic Catholics, and German Catholics.

CHAPTER FIVE

A Natural Place

The Loess Hills Scenic Byway

About a million years ago, during the Ice Age, Iowa would have been hard to find. The Nebraskan glacier was the first to bury the land under a 1-mile (1.6-km)-thick sheet of ice. About 300,000 years later, the Kansan ice pack moved south from Canada. A third glacier, the Illinoisan, approached from the east. The last glacier to touch Iowa, the Wisconsin, covered the northern part of the state barely 11,000 years ago.

The ice sheets shaped the land, flattening the ancient hills like a giant rolling pin. Hundreds of millions of tons of thick, rich topsoil were left behind as the ice melted. The glaciers formed three distinct parts of the state: the Dissected Till Plains, the Young Drift Plains, and the Driftless Area.

Opposite: Malanaphy Springs State Preserve

The Dissected Till Plains

The Dissected Till Plains run across southern Iowa. There, the glaciers left layers of till—soil and stones carved up by rivers and streams over time. Soil blown by the wind is called loess and it spreads over the land like a dark, thick blanket. This soil has formed bluffs along the Missouri River that often reach 300 feet (92 meters). The Loess Hills Scenic Byway runs through one such formation. It is 1 to 15 miles (1.6 to 24 km) wide and 200 miles (322 km) long, stretching from Sioux City, Iowa, to St. Joseph, Missouri.

China is the only other country with such extensive deposits of loess. The Loess Ridge Nature Center in Stone State Park near Sioux City offers recreational trails and programs about this earth formation.

The Young Drift Plains

The Young Drift Plains cover the flatter central and northern sections of Iowa. There, the melting glaciers left even more layers of earth and rocks, called drift, making it one of the best crop-growing regions in North America. Shallow swamps in the area were the remains of lakes formed by glacial water.

Generations of farmers, however, have drained most of this marshland in order to expand their fields. The loss of these wetlands, which soak up rains and floods, has become a problem. After a winter with heavy snows or during the spring rains, rivers overflow their banks and spread out over the agricultural land instead of sinking back into the soil.

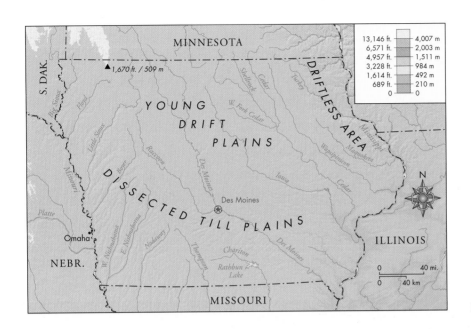

Iowa's topography

Iowa's Geographical Features

Total area; rank	56,276 sq. mi. (145,755 sq km); 26th
Land; rank	55,875 sq. mi. (144,716 sq km); 23rd
Water; rank	401 sq. mi. (1,039 sq km); 42nd
Inland water; rank	401 sq. mi. (1,039 sq km); 36th
Geographic center	Story, 5 miles (8 km) northeast of Ames
Highest point	In Osceola County, 1,670 feet (509 m)
Lowest point	In Lee County, where the Mississippi and Des Moines Rivers merge, 480 feet (146 m)
Largest city	Des Moines
Longest river	Des Moines River, 485 miles (780 km)
Population; rank	2,787,424 (1990 census); 30th
Record high temperature	118°F (48°C) at Keokuk on July 20, 1934
Record low temperature	−47°F (−44°C) at Washta on January 12, 1912
Average July temperature	75°F (24°C)
Average January temperature	19°F (−7°C)
Average annual precipitation	32 inches (81 cm)

Many Iowans enjoy the rugged outdoors.

The Driftless Area

The Driftless Area runs along the Mississippi River. Geologists— scientists who study landforms—say that only one glacier moved through this part of Iowa. As a result, this area was not flattened as much as other parts of the state. This high limestone ridges here have very little topsoil, though, making it hard for farming.

Hikers, hunters, cross-country skiers, and campers love this rugged region, dubbed the Switzerland of Iowa. Downhill skiers take advantage of the 475-foot (145-meters) vertical drop at Sundown Mountain Ski Resort, near Dubuque, the highest drop in Iowa and southern Minnesota.

Iowa Today

Now that all the glaciers are long gone, today's Iowa is much easier to find. It lies in the north-central part of the United States. To the north is Minnesota; to the west is South Dakota and Nebraska. To the east is Wisconsin and Illinois, and Missouri lies to the south. The state covers 56,276 square miles (145,755 square kilometers), which includes 401 square miles (1,039 sq km) of lakes and reservoirs.

Waterways

Iowa's extensive waterways have always been important to the Native Americans and the white settlers who followed them. The

The Mississippi River at Lansing

A Recreation River

A portion of the Missouri River along the Iowa border from Gavins Point Dam at Yankton, South Dakota, to Ponca State Park in Nebraska was designated a National Recreation River in 1978. This part of the river is enjoyed by boaters and fishers who have access from Iowa. It is one of the few stretches of the Missouri that looks much as it did 200 years ago when explorers Lewis and Clark ventured along its banks. ■

rivers helped exploration and commercial development in the state. The Mississippi River forms Iowa's natural eastern border. The Missouri and the Big Sioux Rivers make up the western border, making Iowa the only state bordered on two sides by navigable rivers.

A low ridge called the Mississippi-Missouri Divide runs from Dickinson County in northern Iowa to Davis County in the south. Rivers on the west side of this divide flow into the Missouri and those on the east flow into the Mississippi. The state's eastern rivers are curved; the western rivers are shorter and straighter.

Iowa's longest river is the Des Moines, which runs for 485 miles (780 km), draining about one-quarter of Iowa. The Wapsipinicon, Turkey, Maquoketa, and Cedar Rivers are other major waterways. Smaller rivers include the Skunk, Little Sioux, and Nishnabotna.

Lakes and Reservoirs

Iowa has thirty-one natural lakes. Most were formed by glaciers rather than springs. Clear, East and West Okoboji, Spirit, and

Storm Lakes have long been popular resort areas. West Okoboji is the state's deepest natural lake. The Coralville Reservoir on the Iowa River and the Rathbun Reservoir on the Chariton River provide flood-control basins and recreation on adjacent wildlife preserves. The broad, flat waters of the Red Rock and Saylorville Reservoirs on the Des Moines River are also popular with visitors.

West Okoboji Lake is a resort area that attracts boaters and other tourists.

Highs and Lows

Geographers say that Iowa is part of the Central Lowlands, a great expanse of fertile land between the Appalachian Mountains on the

The Des Moines River, the state's longest river, is part of Dolliver Memorial State Park.

east and the Great Plains on the west. The land is generally flat, especially away from the Mississippi River. Lee County, in the southeastern part of the state, where the Mississippi and Des Moines Rivers merge, is Iowa's lowest point at 480 feet (146 m) above sea level. From here, the landscape slowly rises to the northwest. The highest point in the state is in Osceola County, at 1,670 feet (509 m).

The principal rock types range from soft limestone to shale and

How About Some Frozen Fish?

Iowa's 90,000 acres (36,450 ha) of frozen lakes are great for ice fishing. Ice fishers are three times more likely than summertime fishers to catch a fish. During the winter, most fish gather in the deeper water of the lake's center, making them easier to catch. Ice fishers drill holes through 18 inches (46 cm) of ice and drop in a line. Bluegills, crappies, and perch are prized catches. ■

dolomites. The geode, a stone that has an interior cavity lined with colorful crystals, was adopted as the official state rock in 1967.

All Types of Weather

Iowans say that if you don't like the weather, just wait a minute. Blasts of cold air from the north or hot air from the south can cause swift changes at any time of year. Rapid temperature changes sometimes result in destructive tornadoes.

Iowa generally has hot, muggy summers, perfect for bumper corn harvests. Its long growing season ranges from 170 days in the south to 140 days in the far northwest. Winter can be harsh and blustery with blizzards that roar in from the Great Plains.

Iowa's average July temperature is 75° Fahrenheit (24° Celsius), and its average January temperature is 19°F (–7°C). On January 12, 1912, in Washta, the temperature plummeted to –47°F (–44°C), the lowest mark in the state's recorded history. The state's highest temperature was 118°F (48°C) in Keokuk on July 20, 1934.

Most of Iowa's rain clouds blow up from the south, pushed along the Mississippi River Valley by winds from the Gulf of Mexico. The average annual rainfall is 32 inches (81 centimeters).

Button Up, Muscatine!

Muscatine used to be known as the Pearl Button Capital of the World. The buttons were made from mussel shells dredged up from the bottom of the Mississippi River. In 1905, more than 1.5 billion buttons were made in the city. However, most of today's "pearl" buttons are made of plastic. ■

Iowa's parks and forests

Forests and Flowers

Iowa has more than 2 million acres (810,000 hectares) of forested land classified as commercial land available for growing forest products. Walnut, oak, maple, hickory, cherry, and elm are among the state's hardwoods. Willow trees and cottonwoods fill the river valleys while spruce and fir rise on the rocky ridges of northeastern Iowa. Iowa has four state forests—the Shimek, Stephens, Yellow River, and Loess Hills—and six smaller preserves, totaling 39,328 acres (15,928 ha).

During pioneer days, the tallgrasses of the prairies grew up to 6 feet (1.8 m) high. Today, violets, jack-in-the-pulpits, marsh marigolds, sunflowers, and blue pasqueflowers bloom in the fields. Summertime flowers include the shooting star, purple aven, prairie lily, aster, and wild rose—the state flower. Morel mushrooms grow along parts of the Mississippi River.

Yellow River State Park in winter

Cultivated flowers can also be spectacular. The State Center Rose Garden features hundreds of varieties of roses from May through November. In eastern Iowa, Bellevue's colorful Butterfly Garden attracts more than sixty species of butterflies.

Many ring-necked pheasants are found in Iowa cornfields.

American lotus in bloom at the DeSoto National Wildlife Refuge

Bird Country

Iowa is prime ring-necked pheasant country. In 1998, hunters bagged 1.5 million pheasants. Other game fowl include partridges, turkeys, and quail, some of which are raised in state-run hatcheries and released into the wild.

The Mississippi River Flyway along the eastern border is a great place for bird-watching during migration season. Eagles fly along the waterway all year round, but winter is the best time to see these magnificent birds diving for fish in the water near Dubuque.

In western Iowa's Missouri Valley, the 7,823-acre (3,168-ha) DeSoto National Wildlife Refuge is a stopping place for more than 500,000 snow geese each autumn. The birds stop for rest and food on their annual trek south from the Arctic to nesting grounds in the Gulf of Mexico. Tens of thousands of mallard ducks also visit the refuge. DeSoto researchers have counted as many as 120 bald eagles at one time.

Iowans value nature preservation—and the deer, raccoons, opossums, rabbits, coyotes, and foxes that live in the wild. To protect its natural and historic wonders, Iowa has eighty-three state parks and recreation areas covering nearly 56,000 acres (22,680 ha).

The Palisades Kepler State Park is among the many natural areas that are preserved in Iowa.

CHAPTER SIX

Cities of All Sizes

The best place to start a tour of the Hawkeye State is in the heart of Iowa—Des Moines—the capital city and the state's sports, arts, and government center. The 1990 census counted 193,187 Des Moines residents, making it the state's largest urban area.

The most impressive building in Des Moines is the rectangular state capitol, which features a 275-foot (84-m) gold-leafed dome that reflects the rising and setting sun. In 1964, the 23-carat gold was repaired at a cost of almost $80,000. A ten-year renovation of the entire building was completed, with a price tag of about $41 million. The capitol is known for the grand four-story spiral staircase in its law library. Several of the building's memorials pay tribute to the state's veterans.

Other veterans' memorials located in Des Moines include the 35-foot (11-m) tall, stainless steel Freedom Flame, the centerpiece of a monument to the state's soldiers and sailors, dedicated

The capitol in Des Moines

Opposite: The town of Elkader

Home for a Governor

When Terrace Hill was built in 1869 by Benjamin Franklin Allen, a Des Moines pioneer business-man, locals were amazed by the building's electric lights and steam heating. The house, given to the state in 1971, is now the governor's official home. In 1988, the U.S. Department of the Interior designated the grounds a Natural Backyard Wildlife Habitat.

The house has always been a family place. Most governors already had youngsters when they were elected, but in 1984, Marcus Branstad, son of Governor Terry Branstad and his wife, Chris, became the first child born to a serving governor since 1852. ▪

in 1996. There are also memorials to the Iowans who fought in the Civil, Spanish-American, Korean, and Vietnam Wars.

Another Des Moines attraction is the Minor Basilica of St. John. The domed building has forty-six stained-glass windows as well as intricate plasterwork and wood carvings.

Gold of another kind—corn—is featured at the Iowa State Fair in Des Moines. The entire fairgrounds are on the National Register of Historic Places. It is the state's largest tourist event and attracts hundreds of thousands every summer. Auto racing, horse and dog shows, and arts programs are held there throughout the year.

From Sprint Cars to Rodeos

In south-central Iowa, Knoxville's National Sprint Car Hall of Fame and Museum is the nation's only museum dedicated to the history of sports-car racing. Knoxville is also the home of the Belinda Toy Museum, located in a former church built in 1846.

The Nelson Pioneer Farm Museum in nearby Oskaloosa features many frontier-era buildings. One of the museum's barns is listed on the National Register of Historic Places.

The Woodlands Scenic Byway in the southeast begins in Donnellson. The road curves around farms, historic sites, and several state forests and runs through the typical small Iowa towns of Drakesville, Bloomfield, and Troy. It also passes through Keosauqua, home of the Van Buren County Courthouse, built in 1840—the oldest courthouse in continuous use west of the Mississippi.

To the southwest, Bridgewater is home to the Iowa Aviation Hall of Fame at Greenfield Municipal Airport. For a more ground-level experience, watch the bucking broncos and wild bulls at the Championship Rodeo in Sidney, a town attraction since 1923.

A Grand Interior

The interior of the Iowa capitol has twenty-nine types of imported and domestic marble as well as walnut, cherry, catalpa, butternut, and oak wood from Iowa's forests. Stone for the basement was quarried in Johnson County. Stone for the exterior of the main building came from other Iowa counties. ■

Council Bluffs and Sioux City

North along the Missouri River is Council Bluffs, sometimes called the Crossroads of the American West. Many pioneer trails converged here to cross the Missouri River to Utah, Oregon, and California. The city was the jumping-off point for wagon trains, soldiers, fur traders, settlers, and adventurers. The Western Historic Trails Center displays artifacts used by settlers who stopped at Council Bluffs for supplies before moving on.

The city is full of historic buildings. Among the places to see are the General Dodge House, now a museum, and Kanesville

Inside the General Dodge House in Council Bluffs

The Civic Center in Sioux City

Tabernacle, where Mormon leader Brigham Young was named president of the Church of Jesus Christ of Latter-day Saints. The city's historic Squirrel Cage Jail was built in 1885. It features a cage that rotated to allow jailers to watch the prisoners in their pie-shaped cells from a central point. Also in Council Bluffs is the Lewis and Clark Monument and Scenic Overlook, which honors the famous American explorers.

On the banks of the Missouri River north of Council Bluffs is Sioux City. The city's Sergeant Floyd Riverboat Museum and Welcome Center tells the story of the only person to die on the Lewis and Clark expedition—Charles Floyd, done in apparently by a

Iowa's cities and interstates

ruptured appendix. The center is housed in a refurbished riverboat that the U.S. Army Corps of Engineers used for fifty years during its inspection of the river. On a bluff overlooking the city, a 100-foot (31-m) white stone monument marks Floyd's burial site.

Another towering monument on the Sioux City skyline is a 30-foot (9-m) stainless steel statue of the Immaculate Heart of Mary, Queen of Peace. A statue of the Sacred Heart of Jesus was completed in 1998. Both markers stand on a bluff called Trinity Heights.

Sioux City's Mid-America Air Museum marks the history of flight. It examines military, commercial, and sport aviation.

From Shrines to Trucks

West Bend's Grotto of the Redemption in north-central Iowa is one of the world's largest such structures, hand made from rocks,

gems, and glass. The grotto was established in 1912 by a local priest named Paul Dobberstein. More than 100,000 people visit the shrine every year.

South of West Bend is Fort Dodge. Built in the mid-1860s to guard the frontier, the old fort was one of the most important outposts in the western United States. A replica of the fort has been constructed to house Native American, pioneer, and military artifacts. During the summer, the fort hosts a Frontier Days festival and a Civil War encampment. Fort Dodge is also home to the Blanden Memorial Art Museum, one of the state's first community art museums, which opened in 1932.

One of the largest cities in northern Iowa is Waterloo, home of

The Grotto of the Redemption in West Bend is an elaborate shrine made of rocks and gems.

Deere & Company. Visitors can tour one of the plants to see how a farm tractor is made, from casting its parts in the foundry to the assembly line. Waterloo's Junior Art Galley in the museum of art offers hands-on tours to about 14,000 schoolchildren each year. The Bluedorn Science Imaginarium and the Grout Museum of History and Science provide opportunities for youngsters to learn about pioneer history as well as astronomy and electricity.

Nashua, New Hampton, and Waverly

North of Waterloo is Nashua's Little Brown Church in the Vale, made famous by the nineteenth-century hymn "The Church in the Wildwood." The church is a popular place for weddings. An annual reunion in August brings back hundreds of couples who were married in the old brown building.

In nearby New Hampton, the county seat of Chickasaw County, the former Carnegie Library is now a cultural center. It features the

The Sullivan Brothers

When World War II began, five brothers from Waterloo—Albert, Madison, Joseph, Francis, and George Sullivan—enlisted in the navy. They all ended up serving on the U.S.S. *Juneau.* In 1942, all five young men died when their huge warship went down in the South Pacific. The War Department subsequently ruled that no two members of the same family could serve in the same military unit. The navy later christened the U.S.S. *Sullivan* in their honor.

Waterloo's Sullivan Park incorporates the family home and a memorial. In 1988, the city renamed its convention hall the Five Sullivan Brothers Convention Center. A 1944 movie, *The Fighting Sullivans,* was a box-office hit and was nominated for an Academy Award for best original screenplay. ■

work of local artists and collectors. Permanent displays include an intricate miniature circus built by Richard Natvig, a member of the Circus Model Builders of America, the Tunnell eyeglass collection, the Railroad Room, the Old Toy Shop, and a model train that rides along tracks suspended from the ceiling.

Each spring and autumn, Waverly hosts two of the largest draft-horse auctions in the country. Buyers from around the world look over the prize Belgians, Percherons, and Clydesdales. The horse shows also feature harness auctions and sales of antique horse-drawn farm equipment.

Dubuque and the Quad Cities

Because of its hills, Dubuque looks like a miniature San Francisco. The city is one of the state's oldest. It was named after Julien

A view of Dubuque

Buffalo Bill

Frontier hero Buffalo Bill Cody was born in Scott County in 1846. The Cody family lived in the village of Princeton. Cody's father built a small home there in 1847 and lived in Princeton for several years before moving on. Young Cody became a Pony Express rider at the age of fourteen, carrying mail to outposts in the Far West. He was also an army scout, a buffalo hunter, and an owner of the Buffalo Bill Wild West Show. He died in 1917. ■

Dubuque, a French businessman generally considered Iowa's first white settler. He came to the Midwest in 1788 to mine lead. The lead was used primarily for making musket balls; the boiling lead, dropped from a high building, formed balls as it fell to the ground.

Dubuque's Loras and Clarke Colleges and the University of Dubuque make the city a state educational center. Their students come from around the world.

The Old Jail Art Gallery is housed in Dubuque's old county jail, built in 1858. The Egyptian-style building displays the work of nationally known local artists.

The Quad Cities of Bettendorf and Davenport, Iowa, and Moline and Rock Island, Illinois, are an industrial hub, in a bend on the Mississippi River. The Quad Cities host an annual St. Patrick's Day parade in March. Because the parade starts in Rock Island, Illinois, and crosses a bridge to Iowa, it is considered the only interstate St. Patrick's Day parade in the United States.

Cedar Rapids, Iowa City, and Keokuk

Cedar Rapids, in eastern Iowa's Linn County, is the state's second-largest city with 108,751 residents, according to the 1990 census. The nearby Indian Creek Nature Center has 210 acres (85 ha) of prairies and woods. In early spring, locals come here for the Maple Syrup Festival. The Cedar Greenbelt and the Sauk and Mesquakie national recreation trails cross the center's grounds.

Iowa City, a thriving arts community, is home of the University of Iowa, with its thousands of international students. From 1842 to 1846, Iowa City was the capital of Iowa Territory. It was the state's

first capital from 1846 to 1857. The Old Capitol Museum, an ornate white building with four towering columns, is on the university campus. Just outside the city is the Devonian Fossil Gorge at Coralville Lake, where visitors can see an ancient seabed exposed during the floods of 1993.

The Cedar Rapids skyline

The University of Iowa
is located in Iowa City.

Iowa's most southeastern city is named after the Native American chief Keokuk. Its strategic position at a bend in the Mississippi made it an important Union port during the Civil War. The city was later the site of a huge military hospital.

The Underground Railroad

Before the Civil War, Iowa had many stations on the Underground Railroad—safe houses where runaway slaves from the Southern states could rest on their way to Canada. One station in Iowa was the Lewelling House in Salem in Henry Country, just over the border from Missouri, then a slave state. Escaping slaves often hid in the building's basement. Salem's residents were mostly Quakers whose peace-loving philosophies angered the slave catchers, who threatened to kill them and burn their homes. ▉

The state's only national cemetery is in Keokuk. Congress designated it as a national cemetery in 1862. Confederate and Union soldiers who perished during the American Civil War are buried here side by side.

Keokuk's national cemetery

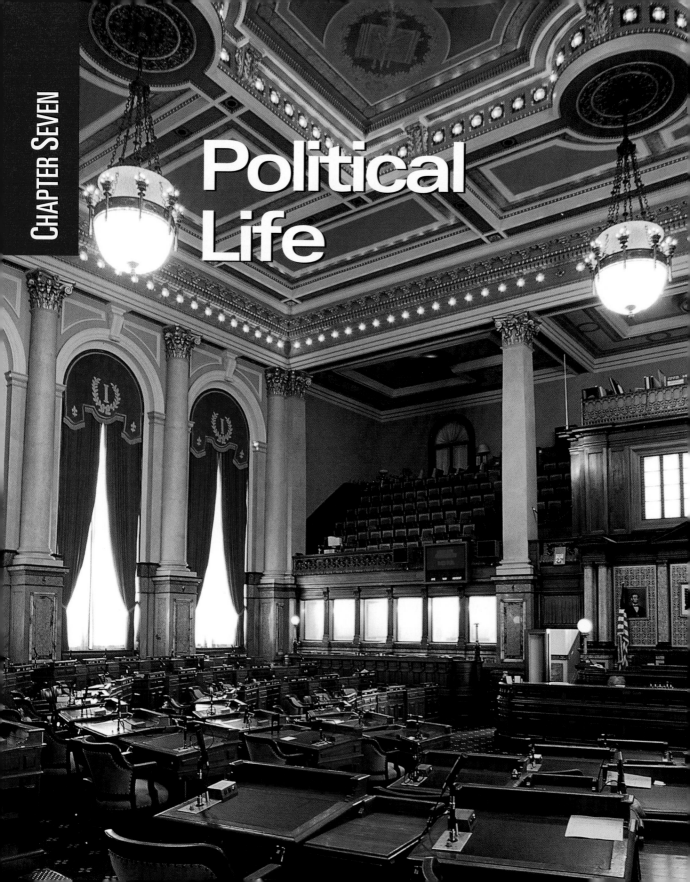

CHAPTER SEVEN

Political Life

A view of downtown Des Moines, Iowa's capital

owans are proud that their state constitution is one of the oldest in use in the United States. The present constitution, adopted in 1857, was preceded by a constitution written in 1846 when Iowa was admitted to the Union. Today's constitution has been amended about forty times over the past century.

An amendment has to be proposed by one of the two houses in the state legislature to change the Iowa constitution. A majority of both houses in the next legislative session must then approve the amendment. Finally, a majority of the voters must approve the amendment.

Executive Branch

The Iowa governor is the state's chief executive, elected to a four-year term, with an unlimited number of terms. The governor shares power with the legislative and judicial branches of government. For instance, he or she can overrule, or veto, a piece of legislation. But

Opposite: The house of representatives chambers within the capitol

Governor Thomas J. Vilsack succeeded Terry Branstad in 1999.

the legislature can override a governor's veto with a two-thirds majority. However, Iowa's governor can also veto parts of financial legislation and approve the rest of the bill. This powerful right is called a line-item veto.

The governor also chairs the state executive council, which consists of the secretary of state, state treasurer, auditor, and secretary of agriculture. The executive council—whose members can be of different political parties—is responsible for the day-to-day operations of state government.

The governor appoints the heads of some twenty administrative departments and agencies who report directly to him. The major departments include revenue, public health, natural resources, general services, management and budget, public safety, human services, education, economic development, and transportation. As a check-and-balance, the legislature must confirm these appointments.

"Governor for Life"

After serving four terms spanning sixteen years, Republican Terry Branstad was sometimes dubbed "governor for life." First elected in 1983, at thirty-seven years old, he was the youngest governor in Iowa history.

Branstad served as a state legislator from 1973 to 1979 and as lieutenant governor from 1979 to 1983. The state's longest-serving governor, Branstad held office until 1998, when he decided against another run. At the end of his last term, he was the senior sitting governor in the United States.

Branstad also took an active role in politics outside Iowa. He was chair of the Republican Governors Conference and the powerful National Governors Association. Branstad grew up on his family's farm near Leland in Winnebago County. ∎

Iowa's Governors

Name	Party	Term	Name	Party	Term
Ansel Briggs	Dem.	1846–1850	George W. Clarke	Rep.	1913–1917
Stephen P. Hempstead	Dem.	1850–1854	William L. Harding	Rep.	1917–1921
James W. Grimes	Whig	1854–1858	N. E. Kendall	Rep.	1921–1925
Ralph P. Lowe	Rep.	1858–1860	John Hammill	Rep.	1925–1931
Samuel J. Kirkwood	Rep.	1860–1864	Daniel W. Turner	Rep.	1931–1933
William M. Stone	Rep.	1864–1868	Clyde L. Herring	Dem.	1933–1937
Samuel Merrill	Rep.	1868–1872	Nelson G. Kraschel	Dem.	1937–1939
Cyrus C. Carpenter	Rep.	1872–1876	George A. Wilson	Rep.	1939–1943
Samuel J. Kirkwood	Rep.	1876–1877	Bourke B. Hickenlooper	Rep.	1943–1945
Joshua G. Newbold	Rep.	1877–1878	Robert D. Blue	Rep.	1945–1949
John H. Gear	Rep.	1878–1882	William S. Beardsley	Rep.	1949–1954
Buren R. Sherman	Rep.	1882–1886	Leo Elthon	Rep.	1954–1955
William Larrabee	Rep.	1886–1890	Leo A. Hoegh	Rep.	1955–1957
Horace Boies	Dem.	1890–1894	Herschel C. Loveless	Dem.	1957–1961
Frank D. Jackson	Rep.	1894–1896	Norman A. Erbe	Rep.	1961–1963
Francis M. Drake	Rep.	1896–1898	Harold E. Hughes	Dem.	1963–1969
Leslie M. Shaw	Rep.	1898–1902	Robert D. Fulton	Dem.	1969
Albert B. Cummins	Rep.	1902–1908	Robert D. Ray	Rep.	1969–1983
Warren Garst	Rep.	1908–1909	Terry E. Branstad	Rep.	1983–1999
Beryl F. Carroll	Rep.	1909–1913	Thomas J. Vilsack	Dem.	1999–

Thirty Iowa governors have been Republicans. Only ten have been Democrats. James W. Grimes, governor from 1854 to 1858, was a member of the Whig Party. Although third parties such as the Reform Party have made some inroads recently, Iowa is truly a two-party state, with Democrats and Republicans vying for power.

No woman has ever been elected governor in Iowa. However, in 1986, the people elected JoAnn Zimmerman as its first female

Sally Pederson followed two other women as lieutenant governor.

A Mural That Tells the Iowa Story

Westward, a mural in the Iowa capitol, symbolizes the forward movement of settlers into Iowa. The painting, created by Edwin H. Blashfield in 1904, shows a family riding in a wagon and other set- tlers coming through a field of corn. Figures representing agri- culture and technology float over- head. A buffalo skull on the left side of the picture represents the prairie. ■

lieutenant governor. Joy Corning, who worked as a state senator and schoolteacher, became the state's second female lieutenant governor in 1990 and was reelected in 1994. She also served as chair of the National Conference of Lieutenant Governors. Demo- crat Sally Pederson was elected to the post in 1998.

The final member of the executive branch of government is the attorney general, the state's chief legal officer. The attorney general heads the Iowa Department of Justice. One of the depart- ment's most important units is the Consumer Protection Division.

Iowa's State Government

Executive Branch

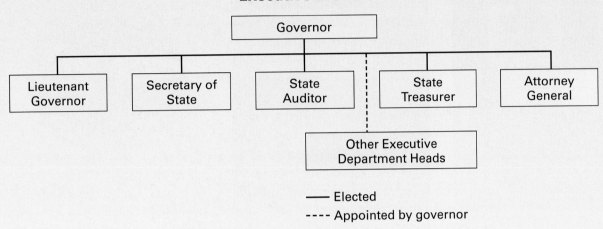

Governor

Lieutenant Governor | Secretary of State | State Auditor | State Treasurer | Attorney General

Other Executive Department Heads

—— Elected

---- Appointed by governor

Legislative Branch

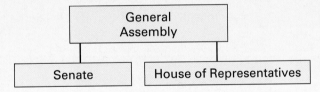

General Assembly

Senate | House of Representatives

Judicial Branch

Supreme Court

Court of Appeals

District Courts

Iowa's State Flag and Seal

Iowa was about seventy-five years old when it finally adopted a state flag. Before World War I, Iowa National Guardsmen were stationed along the Texas-Mexico border without any state flag, inspiring the Daughters of the American Revolution to design a banner. The state legislature adopted it in 1921. According to Dixie Cornell Gebhardt of Knoxville, who developed the final design, the flag has three vertical bars: blue for loyalty, justice, and truth; white for purity; and red for courage. In the center is an eagle carrying a streamer inscribed with the state motto.

The seal depicts a soldier standing in a wheat field surrounded by farming and industrial equipment with the Mississippi River in the background. At the top, an eagle holds a streamer on which the state motto is written. The seal was adopted in 1847. ■

Iowa's State Symbols

State flower: Wild rose Found throughout Iowa, the wild rose (left) was adopted by the Iowa General Assembly in 1897. That same year, wild rose was a decoration on the silver service the state gave to the U.S.S. *Iowa*.

State bird: Eastern goldfinch This bird was adopted in 1933. Found across the state throughout the year, the eastern goldfinch feeds on the seeds of a variety of plants.

State tree: Oak At least one type of oak tree is found in every area of Iowa. Adopted in 1961 as the state's official tree, the oak is important to many kinds of wildlife.

State rock: Geode Known for its abundance of geodes, the Iowa legislature chose the geode as the state rock in 1967. Found in limestone, geodes are spherical stones lined with beautiful mineral crystals. ■

Iowa's State Song
"Song of Iowa"
Words by S. H. M. Byers

During his imprisonment by the Confederate army during the Civil War, S. H. M. Byers often heard the Southern song "My Maryland" sung to the tune of "*Die Tannenbaum.*" He composed his own words for that song in 1897.

*You ask what land I love the best,
  Iowa, 'tis Iowa
The fairest state in all the west,
  Iowa, O! Iowa
From yonder Mississippi's stream*

*To where Missouri's waters gleam,
O fair it is as poet's dream, Iowa,
  O! Iowa*

*See yonder fields of tasseled
  corn, Iowa, 'tis Iowa
Where plenty fills her golden
  horn, Iowa, in Iowa
See how her wondrous praises
  shine
To yonder sunset's purpling line
O happy land, O! land of mine,
  Iowa, O! Iowa.*

Legislative Branch

The second branch of Iowa government is the state legislature, called the General Assembly. It is divided into a senate of fifty members and a house of representatives of one hundred members. Senators serve four-year terms; representatives serve two-year terms.

Both houses meet regularly about one hundred days a year, with the opening session on the second Monday in January. The legislature or the governor can call emergency special sessions. The state house and senate are responsible for making the laws that run the state.

Judicial Branch

Iowa's judicial branch of government is made up of its courts. The state supreme court is the highest court in the state. Its nine justices are appointed by the governor to eight-year terms. The governor selects from a list of three candidates submitted by a state judicial nominating commission. The justices choose a chief justice from their group.

Iowa also has a court of appeals with statewide jurisdiction. This court has six judges, who serve six-year terms.

Each of the state's eight judicial districts also has a court, with a minimum of six judges and a maximum of twenty. These judges, who have six-year terms, are also appointed by the governor. But after serving as appointees for one year, judges must run for election.

Revenue and Spending

Iowa raises money through gambling revenue, sales taxes, corporate and individual taxes, inheritance tax, and cigarette, tobacco, and liquor taxes. Motor vehicle taxes help pay for highway maintenance.

Iowa has ninety-nine counties, each of which has an elected board of supervisors of three to five members. Almost every county has something to brag about. For example, Chickasaw County pitches itself as the Petunia Capital of Iowa and for years has sponsored an annual Petunia Festival in the county seat of New Hampton.

County officers include the county sheriff, attorney, treasurer, auditor, recorder, assessor, and engineer. There is also a

Iowa's counties

social welfare board. Counties keep important records, maintain rural roads and bridges, administer social services, and handle law enforcement.

Managing Iowa's Cities

Iowa has 949 cities, ranging from sprawling Des Moines to tiny Delphos. According to the 1990 census, 498 cities in Iowa have fewer than 500 residents.

Although a few cities have a manager, most have a mayor-council form of government that is responsible for local administration. Cities raise money for various projects by property taxes, licenses and fees, revenue from the state, and contracts for services.

At the Federal Level

Iowa has two U.S. senators and five U.S. representatives in Congress. Over the years, Iowa congressional leaders have held important positions.

In one of the most recent displays of statesmanship, Democratic senator Tom Harkin was a major voice in the 1999 impeachment trial of President Bill Clinton. He urged compromise and nonpartisanship in the debates over whether to remove the president from office. Before he was elected to the U.S. Senate, Harkin represented Iowa in the U.S. House of Representatives from 1975 to 1985. In 1992, he ran for the Democratic presidential nomination.

The Iowa Caucus

Iowans are proud of their caucus (or primary) system which is one of the first tests for national presidential candidates from both

Senator Tom Harkin

The Home of Herbert Hoover

President Herbert Hoover (1874–1964) was born in West Branch. His father, a blacksmith, died when he was six years old, and his mother had to support the family. When Herbert's mother died four years later, he went to live with several uncles. Herbert Hoover eventually became a mining engineer and headed relief efforts in Europe after World War I. Later he served as secretary of commerce in the Warren G. Harding administration. He became the thirty-first president in 1929.

Herbert Hoover is best remembered for being president at the start of the worldwide financial calamity called the Great Depression. "Hoovervilles" were shantytowns where desperately poor people lived at the edges of cities during the depression. Hoover's home in West Branch is now a museum (above). ■

White House Wives from Iowa

Born in Waterloo in 1874, Lou Henry Hoover (above), wife of Herbert Hoover, was independent and resourceful. She was the first woman to earn a geology degree from Stanford University, where she met her husband, the future thirty-first president of the United States. Throughout her married life, Mrs. Hoover was involved in public causes such as education for women and public housing. She twice served as president of the Girl Scouts of America, and organized the National Women's Athletic Association and the National Women's Conference on Law Enforcement. She died in 1944 and was elected to the Iowa Women's Hall of Fame in 1987.

Born in Boone in 1896, Mamie Doud Eisenhower (bottom left), wife of Dwight D. Eisenhower, lived in Cedar Rapids until her family moved to Colorado. Her first pet was a lamb that had to be given away when it grew into a large ram. As a child, she loved playing "dress up," and as an adult, she was consistently named one of the ten best-dressed women in the United States. Mrs. Eisenhower was one of the country's most popular first ladies.

In 1916, Mamie married the dashing young Eisenhower after his graduation from West Point Military Academy. He went on to command U.S. forces in Europe during World War II and was elected president in 1952. After taking the oath of office, Eisenhower gave Mamie a big kiss—it was the first time a president was seen kissing his wife in public!

Mamie Eisenhower died in 1979 and was named to the Iowa Women's Hall of Fame in 1993. Her restored home in Boone is now open to the public. ■

parties. Every presidential election year, Iowa's Democrats and Republicans hold meetings in 2,500 precincts to vote on which candidate to support.

Since the Iowa caucus system is one of the first steps in the national presidential campaign, the state is full of candidates eager to attract the attention of state convention delegates. Doing well in Iowa

Presidential candidate Phil Gramm on his campaign bus in Iowa during the 1996 Republican primary

means media attention and financial contributions, which are increasingly necessary to run a national campaign. On the other hand, a poor showing in Iowa can be a major setback for a politician's bid for the White House.

From Corn to Computers

Agriculture has been Iowa's major industry since the settlers crossed the Mississippi with sharpened plows and bags of seed. Today, giant tractors equipped with air conditioners, computers, and stereos lumber across the fields.

The state has some 33.2 million acres (13.4 million ha) of farmland, and farming is a big business, generating nearly $12 billion annually. Iowa is a leading producer of beef, corn, and pork.

One-fourth of all of the nation's hogs come from Iowa. Iowa farms also raise 20 percent of the country's corn and 18 percent of its soybeans. When it comes to the value of its agricultural products, Iowa ranks second behind California. Iowa's fertile fields also grow sorghum, oats, barley, wheat, rye, flaxseed, sunflowers, hay, peas, lentils, potatoes, and sweet potatoes.

Opposite: A cornfield outside Lone Rock

A young crop of soybeans

Family Farmers

Iowa's family farms are essential to the survival and success of the state, but managing a farm is tough and stressful. Farmers have to deal with drought, floods, tornadoes, and pests as well as the need for expensive new equipment and techniques. They also have to consider environmental questions, such as whether to use pesticides, growth hormones, and fertilizers or adopt organic methods.

What Iowa Grows, Manufactures, and Mines

Agriculture	Manufacturing	Mining
Beef cattle	Chemicals	Limestone
Corn	Electrical equipment	Sand and gravel
Hogs	Food products	
Soybeans	Machinery	
	Printed materials	

A Russian Visitor

In 1959, Nikita S. Khrushchev, then premier of the former Soviet Union, came to Iowa to see first-hand how its farmers could produce such an abundance of quality crops. Roswell Garst of Coon Rapids, who was one of the world's largest producers of hybrid seed corn at that time, hosted the premier.

Khrushchev visited the Garst farm at the height of the Cold War, the ideological conflict between the United States and the Soviet Union. But Garst, a shrewd businessman, was also a caring, concerned Iowan who wanted to share his knowledge and help alleviate world hunger. Today, families can stay overnight at the Garsts' home to watch cows being milked and animals fed. ■

Much of what happens in the agriculture industry is beyond the control of the local farmer. Prices for harvested crops may drop because of a national oversupply. Competition from other states and other countries affects sales too. Huge corporations own "factory

Family farming in Iowa

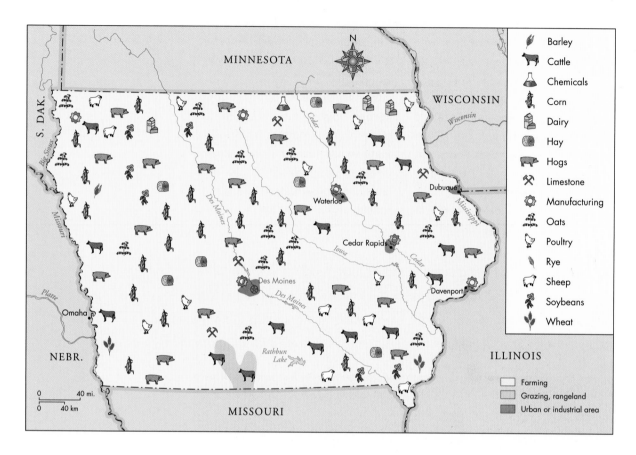

Iowa's natural resources

farms," where thousands of animals are raised at one time. Because of their size, these corporations can control pricing and distribution of products. All these challenges take their toll on the small farmer, whose numbers have dropped steadily over the past fifty years. And fewer young people are staying in the family business.

The size of family farms has also decreased. In 1938, the Adams Ranch in Sac County, with more than 7,000 acres (2,835 ha), was Iowa's largest family farm. Today, the average size of the family farm is 339 acres (137 ha), although some are 500 acres (203 ha) or more. An economic crunch in the 1980s

Hamburger Corn Bake

Iowa is famous for its corn and beef, featured in this dish.

Ingredients:

1 1/2 pounds hamburger

1 cup onions, chopped

3 cups noodles, medium sized

12 ounces corn, frozen or fresh

1 can cream of chicken soup

1 can cream of mushroom soup

1 cup sour cream

1/2 cup pimentos, chopped

1/2 teaspoon salt

1/2 tablespoon pepper

2 tablespoons butter, melted

1/2 cup breadcrumbs

Directions:

Cook the hamburger and onions together in a saucepan, until the meat is brown and the onions are cooked.

In a separate pot, boil the noodles until done. Drain and add the cooked noodles to the hamburger. Stir in other ingredients, except for butter and breadcrumbs. Place the mixture in a casserole dish.

Combine breadcrumbs with melted butter in a separate bowl and layer over top of hamburger mixture.

Bake in preheated oven at 350°F for about 45 minutes.

Serves 4–6.

Winner of a Nobel Prize

After World War II, countries around the world turned their attention to feeding their people. Seeds resistant to heat, insects, and other perils were in demand. Norman Borlaug (above), born in Cresco, Iowa, developed fast-growing strains of hardy crops. For his success in increasing food production, he was awarded the Nobel Peace Prize in 1970. ■

Soil erosion had a terrible effect on many Iowa farms.

drove many farmers who couldn't pay their bills out of business. And big corporations were often standing by ready to snap up their land at bargain prices.

Land Preservation

After more than a century of farming, by the 1960s, Iowa had lost almost half of its rich topsoil. Wind and water erosion had taken its toll, as more advanced tilling churned deeper and deeper into the black loam. It is estimated that when the first settlers cut the prairie sod, the topsoil was 3 to 5 feet (1 to 1.5 meters) deep in places. Today, it is only about 2 feet (61 cm) deep.

In recent decades, more efficient farming methods have been developed. In 1972, university extension agents in Iowa established the nation's first state Soil Conservation Cost-Share Program, which partially repays farmers for restoring and preserving their land. In 1980, the Iowa Soil 2000 Program set up a twenty-year schedule for applying soil-erosion prevention measures. The state also passed numerous environmental-protection bills to preserve the groundwater. Iowa spends more than $3 million

A (Delicious) Apple a Day

The famous red Delicious apple was developed on a farm near East Peru. In the 1880s, Jesse Hiatt noticed shoots springing from a wild apple tree stump on his property. They produced a fruit that he had never tasted before, so he nurtured the tree and entered its apples in a contest in 1895. His apple, which he called the Hawkeye, won the contest. The Stark Brothers Nursery quickly bought the rights to grow the apple and renamed it the Delicious. It is now the best-selling apple in the United States. Shoots from the original tree still produce apples on Hiatt's old farm. ■

annually on research and education projects to decrease the use of chemicals in farming.

Farmers are also encouraged to diversify their crops. Diversifying not only preserves the soil but protects against market fluctuations. Flowers and Christmas trees are two successful examples of Iowa's farms branching out. In addition, the state works closely with the federal government to encourage the establishment of farmers' markets in poor city neighborhoods. Fifty-seven such markets were operating during the harvesting season of 1998.

The state also labels many products with its "Iowa Grown for You" label. It is a mark of quality that consumers trust.

More Than Agriculture

Iowa is not just an agricultural state. In fact, only about 8 percent of the state's workers are farmers. Today, 50 percent are employed in the service sector, which includes education, banking, medicine, and retail trade.

Many of the state's industries draw on Iowa's close connection with agriculture. Companies produce a range of food products including popcorn, bacon, oatmeal, jelly, and pressed meats. Quaker Oats operates one of the world's largest cereal mills in Cedar Rapids, capable of turning out 30 million cases a year, each weighing 14 pounds (6.4 kilograms).

In the 1970s and 1980s, economic slumps forced some heavy-equipment companies to close, and thousands of workers lost their jobs. But by the 1990s, a booming national economy encouraged

businesses to expand. Hunt-Wesson Foods opened a $60 million pudding plant in Waterloo. Heinz Corporation, the ketchup producer, spent $1 million to enlarge a plant in Muscatine. Swiss Valley Farms expanded its fluid-milk plant in Dubuque at a cost of $5.5 million.

Iowa makes rubber and plastic products, electronics, pharmaceuticals, and machinery. Winnebago recreation vehicles are produced in Forest City. Cayel Craft makes ambulances in Rock Rapids. In Orange City, Angel Aircraft designs and manufactures small planes for bush-pilot missionaries in remote areas of the

The Quaker Oats building in Cedar Rapids

Deere & Company,
famous for its tractors,
is a significant
presence throughout
the nation.

world. Amana Refrigeration is a leader in energy-efficient cooling and heating equipment. Deere & Company produces agricultural equipment, ranging from corn pickers to lawn tractors. Ralston-Purina, the world's largest pet-food manufacturer, began work in the late 1990s on a five-year, $22.6 million project to expand its Clinton and Davenport plants.

The Iowa Department of Economic Development assists companies by helping them qualify for state aid and tax credits. The state's universities help the business sector develop better products and train workers more efficiently. The University of Iowa's Technological Innovation Center even provides laboratory and office space for start-up technology firms.

Service Industries

Service industries bring in about 68 percent of Iowa's annual gross product—the total value of goods and services produced by a state in a year. Industry brings in 28 percent, and farming, 4 percent. Wholesale selling and servicing of farm machinery are among the most profitable service companies. Automobile dealerships, grocery stores, and restaurants lead in retail sales. Insurance, banking, and real estate are the next largest segments of the service industry. Des Moines is one of the nation's insurance centers. Principal Mutual Life, one of the largest insurance firms in the United States, is headquartered here.

Gambling

Gambling is now one of Iowa's principal sources of state revenue. Floating casinos opened in the early 1990s. It was hoped that the gambling industry would spur economic development in Marquette, Fort Madison, Dubuque, and Davenport, where players are attracted from surrounding states. Altoona's Prairie Meadows Racetrack and the Bluffs Run Casino in Council Bluffs are just two of the state's many gambling establishments. Iowa also has a state lottery.

Economic Links and Roads

Iowa is in the heart of an eight-state market with 840,000 businesses and 34.2 million potential consumers with billions of dollars to spend. The state's early business leaders knew that Iowa's location would be the key to its success and understood the importance of close links with the rest of the United States. In 1893, Iowa built the nation's first reinforced concrete bridge. In the late 1800s, a pontoon railroad bridge linked Marquette, Iowa, to Prairie du Chien, Wisconsin. It wasn't long before the state's cities were connected by road.

In 1917, the state launched an impressive road-building program, hiring major contractors such as New Hampton's Albert Russell, who used mule-drawn drags—heavy metal rakes used to flatten dirt or break up clots—to improve rural roads. In the early days of auto travel, Highway 6—a ribbon of concrete between Des Moines and Council Bluffs—was nicknamed the Great White Way.

The Lincoln Highway was the first paved transcontinental highway to cross Iowa. The highway is now known as Highway 30. Today, multilane interstate highways divide the state. The east-west I-80 corridor is one of the busiest, handling tens of thousands of trucks and cars per day. I-35 is a major north-south roadway.

Interstate 80, where it crosses the Mississippi River from Illinois into Iowa

Although traveling by railroads is now almost a thing of the past, trains once brought a flood of people to the state. Abraham Lincoln chose Council Bluffs as the eastern junction of the first transcontinental railroad.

And the country's shortest railroad, the Fenelon Place Elevator, is in Dubuque. The track is 296 feet (90 m) long and rises steeply to 189 feet (58 m). J. K. Graves, a local banker, built the railway in 1882 to get from the Mississippi River to the top of a bluff.

J. K. Graves built the Fenelon Place Elevator.

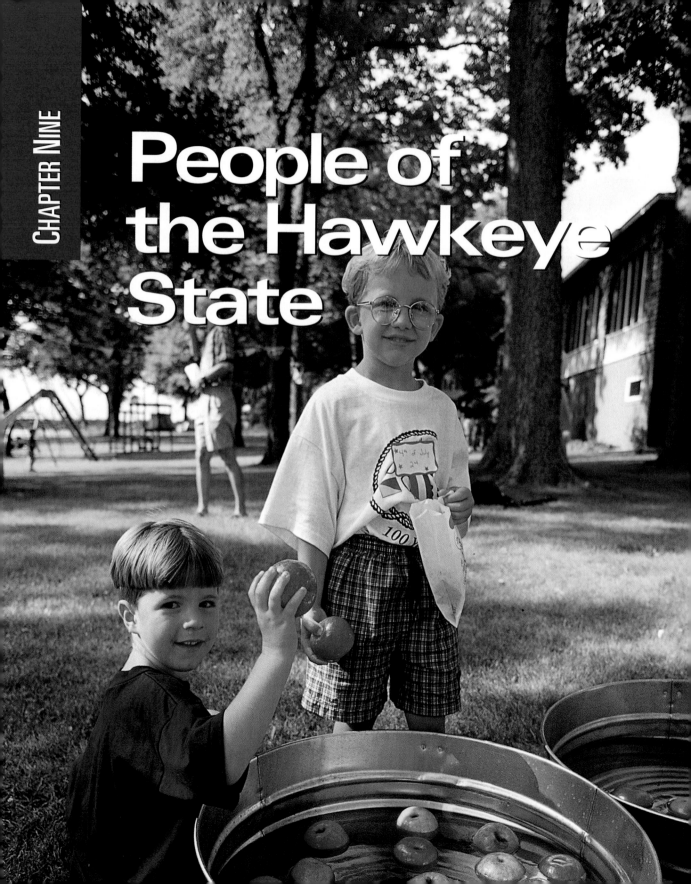

CHAPTER NINE

People of the Hawkeye State

bout 80 percent of Iowa's residents were born in the state. At the end of the 1990s, only 2 percent were foreign-born, unlike the late 1800s when almost half the people were immigrants, mostly from Europe. Iowa's first settlers were U.S. citizens from eastern and southern states.

Fort Atkinson during the 1840s

However, generations before statehood, Iowa was heavily populated by Native American groups. In the 1840s, Fort Atkinson in northeast Iowa was built to separate the Sioux from their Sauk and Mesquakie enemies and to preserve peace on the frontier. It was the only such military post in the United States. Eventually, most of the Native Americans left Iowa, pushed out by U.S. government treaties and white settlers.

Now, most of the Indians in the state are Mesquakie. In a pact made with the state government, the Mesquakie collected $735 and bought their own land in the 1850s. They eventually purchased some 3,200 acres (1,296 ha) from the state of Iowa. So the Mesquakie still live on their own private land along the Iowa River—not on a reservation. Most Native American populations in other parts of the United States live on reservations assigned by the U.S. government.

Opposite: Iowans enjoying their state's apples

Hawkeye State Honors Black Hawk

One of Iowa's nicknames is the Hawkeye State. The name honors the famous Sauk chief Black Hawk, who led a band of Indians against the whites in the Black Hawk War of 1832. The Indians were defeated and forced to give up their lands along the Mississippi River. This section of Iowa, known as the Black Hawk Purchase, was the first area opened to settlers in 1833. ■

Immigrants

Large numbers of Irish, Germans, Bohemians, Dutch, Norwegians, Danes, and Swedes rounded out the population of early Iowa. Many were attracted to Iowa because of the state's ninety-six-page booklet, printed in 1869 and entitled *Iowa: The Home for Immigrants*. The small booklet, published in English, German,

Many immigrants ventured into Iowa during the nineteenth century.

Dutch, Swedish, and Danish, told about the wonders of living in Iowa.

Eager Europeans came first to New York or Canada on sailing ships. Most traveled west by railroad, but many sailed along the St. Lawrence River through the Great Lakes. Port cities such as Kenosha, Wisconsin, and Chicago, Illinois, welcomed thousands of newcomers. From there, they moved on to Iowa, where their farming skills were put to good use.

A Tale of Two Immigrant Families

Some Iowa families have interesting stories about their journey to Iowa. Patrick Russell came from Ireland as a teenager and made his way to Wisconsin through Canada. He was looking for relatives who had already settled near Erin, an Irish settlement north of Milwaukee. Russell got off a steamer in Kenosha, Wisconsin—the wrong city! He had to walk 40 miles (64 km) north to find his relations. After farming in Wisconsin for several years, he eventually moved west to farm near Lawler, Iowa.

Bridget O'Malley was a young Irish girl who worked as a maid for a wealthy French fur trader in Prairie du Chien, Wisconsin, directly across the Mis-

sissippi River from Iowa. Louis Larson, who emigrated from Bergen, Norway, as a young man, lived on the Iowa side. Larson opened a store in Marquette, Iowa, and soon met Miss O'Malley. In the winter, Larson skated across the river to court her. In the summer, he used his tiny sailboat, the *Bluebird*, to visit. They eventually married and also settled in Lawler, where Larson opened another store.

Since Lawler was such a small town, the Larson and Russell families knew each other. Eventually, one of the Russell sons, Albert, married Gertrude, one of the Larson daughters.

Over the next three genera-

tions, some descendants of the Russell-Larsons remained in Iowa and some were scattered throughout the world. They became judges, social workers, nurses, farmers, actors, artists, fashion models, poets, fair managers, policemen, lumberyard operators, journalists, priests, librarians, engineers, politicians, nuns, and union organizers. One of them was a leading supplier of bucking broncos for rodeos.

A grandson of Albert and Gertrude, Tom Russell, became a well-known folk singer and composer. In 1999, he made an award-winning album, *The Man from God Knows Where*, with songs about his relatives who settled in America. ■

People of the Hawkeye State **103**

After the Civil War, the state's population boomed. The number of residents grew from 674,913 in 1860 to 1,194,020 in 1870. In 1880, the foreign-born population reached 261,650.

Of European Heritage

Although the state has a variety of ethnic groups, most citizens are still of German, Irish, British, or Scandinavian heritage. Many of the earliest arrivals came with their families. They eventually set up businesses, published newspapers, built churches, and established schools, among many other things.

The Vesterheim Norwegian-American Museum in Decorah tells the story of northern Iowa's Norwegian community. When the king and queen of Norway visit the United States, they always stop at the museum to talk with the descendants of the first Norwegian settlers, who still live in the area.

After 1900, many immigrants came from southern and eastern Europe. Italians and Croatians became coal miners in the southern part of the state. Unlike the previous arrivals, these mostly young, single males had no skills. They were often supported by their families back home. Others had to repay money that sponsors had loaned them to come to America. Life in the mining camps was rough, but it gave them a chance for a better life. Once established in Iowa, their relatives often joined them.

Celebrating Iowa's Dutch heritage at the Pella Tulip Time festival

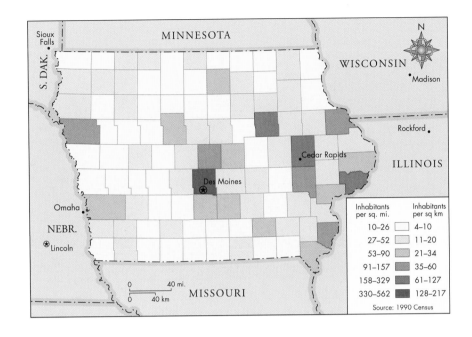

Iowa's population density

African-Americans

Although they make up only about 1.7 percent of today's Iowans, African-Americans have long been part of Iowa. After the Civil War, a few freed slaves came to Iowa to farm. Some of their descendants live in the southeastern part of the state.

Some African-Americans who came to Iowa at the end of the 1800s went to work in the mines, often as strikebreakers hired by the mine owners. After the dirty, backbreaking work underground, there wasn't much for the men to do. But baseball was popular and each mining camp usually had several teams, including the Buxton Wonders, a black team from Buxton in northern Monroe County. More than half of Buxton's 5,000 residents were black. The town existed from 1900 to 1922, when the coal seams ran out.

By the 1950s, all the state's mines were closed. Many African-

Buxton was a mining town in the early 1900s.

Population of Iowa's Major Cities (1990)

Des Moines	193,187
Cedar Rapids	108,751
Davenport	95,333
Sioux City	80,505
Waterloo	66,467
Iowa City	59,738

American families moved to larger cities where jobs in factories and in other industries were plentiful.

African-American women have contributed in many ways to the well-being of the state. In 1930, Gwendolyn Wilson Fowler of Des Moines was the first African-American woman pharmacist licensed in Iowa. Catherine G. Williams was a professional dancer for thirteen years before she went into social welfare. Starting as a typist with the Iowa Department of Social Services, she worked her way up to deputy commissioner. During her thirty-year career, Williams conducted the first statewide training program for foster parents of retarded children and wrote the department's first foster-care study. Ruth Bluford Anderson, associate professor of social work at the University of Northern Iowa, has received recognition for her work in the mental health and substance-abuse fields. Attorney Willie Stevenson Glanton of Des Moines was the first African-American woman elected to the Iowa state legislature. She served from 1965 to 1967 and went on to become president of the Iowa Chapter of the American Bar Association.

Other Minority Groups

According to 1997 government figures, Iowa has only 53,092 residents of Hispanic descent, mostly from Mexico and Central America. The 1990 census recorded 32,643 persons originally from Latin America. Hispanics make up 1.18 percent of the total population.

Iowans also came from the Philippines, India, China, Pakistan, Japan, and countries in Southeast Asia. According to 1997 government figures, 35,778 Asians live in the state, making up just under 1 percent of the population.

Most of Iowa's nonwhite residents live in large urban areas such as Des Moines, Davenport, Cedar Rapids, Waterloo, and Sioux City. While the majority of state residents are Protestant and Catholic, a growing number are Muslims or Buddhists, or belong to other non-Christian faiths.

Minority students at Iowa State University

A Different Way of Life

Over the years, Iowa's rich farmland and reputation as a place to raise families far from the urban frenzy of the East Coast attracted

Amish children work on their family's farm in Hazleton.

small religious groups and "utopians." Utopians sought an ideal area to practice their religion or different lifestyles. Members of these groups often shared all their property and lived a community-centered life that dated back generations.

The Amish settled around Kalona, Hazleton, and Cresco, where their horse-drawn buggies still clop along the rural roads. The Mennonite Museum and Archives in Kalona showcases this denomination's interesting Old World culture and lifestyles.

The Amana Colonies

The Community of True Inspiration was formed in southern Germany in 1714. Typical of many religious sects of its time, the group wanted to worship as they pleased. Because of persecution, they left the Old World to establish new lives in America. In 1842, after a forty-day voyage across the Atlantic Ocean, the first members of the community arrived in America.

Led by Christian Metz, the group made their way to Iowa after spending a few years in New York state. They bought 26,000 acres (10,530 ha) in east-central Iowa and built seven villages about an hour's ox-cart drive apart. Each village had its own shops, farms, churches, and workshops. The 1,200 original settlers owned all property communally, so the community took care of everyone's food, clothing, and housing. The quality goods made by these skilled craftworkers were easily sold to their neighbors.

Over the years, times changed and it became more and more difficult for the seven villages to stay independent. To allow more economic opportunity for individual members, the community voted to separate its religious and financial interests in 1932. This decision, known as the Great Change, marked a new openness to the world.

Today, the Amana Colonies (above) are a tourist attraction and a National Historic Landmark. As in the old days, colony craftworkers make furniture, woolens, clocks, bread, and wine, and sell their products to thousands of visitors. Their members still worship in the old way. Elders rather than ministers lead the prayer services, and men sit on one side of the church while women sit on the other side. ■

Public Education

Regardless of their religious affiliation or ancestry, Iowans have always known the importance of education. The state's Department of Education was created in 1913 to supervise the state's public schools.

From the 1970s through the 1990s, Iowa's youngsters always ranked first or second in the nation in the American College Testing (ACT) and Scholastic Aptitude Tests (SAT). Today, 88 percent of Iowa's students graduate from high school, compared to a national average of 71 percent.

The University of Northern Iowa is in Cedar Falls.

Iowa has three state universities. The University of Iowa was chartered in 1847 within the first two months of statehood. Some 28,000 students from around the world attend the university. Iowa State University—called Iowa State University of Science and Technology since 1959—was created in 1858. Its current enrollment is 25,000 students. The University of Northern Iowa, founded in 1876, specializes in teacher training.

In the mid-1990s, Iowa had twenty public and forty-one private institutions of higher learning. Iowa is also home to the Iowa Braille and Sight-Saving School and the Iowa School for the Deaf.

The Iowa Award

Many famous personalities have been born or lived in Iowa. In 1948, the Iowa Centennial Memorial Foundation established the Iowa Award. It is the state's highest honor, given to individuals

Simon Estes won the Iowa Award in 1996.

Iowan Carrie Lane Chapman Catt fought for women's right to vote.

who have distinguished themselves in their careers. The award is only given every five years to honor "outstanding ability, service and achievement by Iowans." In 1951, the first recipient was President Herbert Hoover. Among the most recent was Simon Estes, an internationally known opera singer, who received the award in 1996.

Other noted recipients included social reformer and women's suffragette Carrie Lane Chapman Catt; chemist Frank Spedding; rocket scientist James Van Allen; U.S. vice president Henry A. Wallace; First Lady Mamie Eisenhower; bandleader Karl King; crop geneticist and Nobelist Norman Borlaug; director of the National Catholic Rural Life Conference, Monsignor Luigi Liguitti; pollster George Gallup; musician Meredith Willson; and Pulitzer Prize–winning newspaper cartoonist Jay Darling.

Iowa Women

In 1975, the Iowa Commission on the Status of Women established the Iowa Women's Hall of Fame to honor women who have helped shape and strengthen Iowa. Among the first recipients was Amelia Jenks Bloomer, a nineteenth-century advocate of women's rights. She is perhaps best remembered for popularizing "the bloomer," an outfit that consisted of a skirt worn over long loose trousers. Ola Babcock Miller became Iowa's first female secretary of state in 1932. She was instrumental in starting the Iowa State Patrol, the state's highway law-enforcement agency. Mary Louise Smith was the first woman to chair the Republican Party.

Amelia Jenks Bloomer wearing her creation

CHAPTER TEN

Crooners, Actors, and Ballplayers

owa is a state that appreciates music, art, dance, theater, and sports. It has eighty arts agencies, nine major art museums, sixty-five theater groups, eighteen music and dance associations, and forty musical groups. Each year, state residents attend more than 160 art fairs and festivals—which can mean big money for the state. For every public dollar spent on the arts, $300 is generated locally. Thousands of fans attend school, amateur, and semi-pro sporting events, such as Drake University's internationally recognized annual track competition in Des Moines. And droves of classical-music enthusiasts attend performances by the Des Moines Metro Opera and the Ames International Orchestra Association.

The Drake University Relays is a well-known track competition.

Iowa has a tradition of classical music. In 1893, Antonín Dvořák the Czech composer, visited relatives and friends in the Bohemian community of Spillville. In this northeastern Iowa village, Dvořák composed his American String Quartet in F Major, in which he combined Native American and African-American themes with traditional Eastern European music.

Many entertainment personalities were born in the state or once called it home. Rock and roll's the Everly Brothers got their radio start on KMA radio in Shenandoah in the 1960s. Crooner

Opposite: Folk musicians at the Scott County Fair

Andy Williams was born in Wall Lake in 1927. He has been a regular feature on television and the club circuit since the 1960s. Musician Bix Beiderbecke (1903–1931) of Davenport inspired an annual jazz festival there named for him. Audubon native C. W. McCall wrote "Convoy," a smash pop song in the 1970s. Iowa was an inspiration even to outsiders. Cowboy star Gene Autry had a hit single with "Sioux City Sue."

Big-band leader Glenn Miller was born in Clarinda in 1904. His music inspired a generation of swing dancers during World War II. *The Glenn Miller Story*, a film starring Jimmy Stewart, was made in 1953. Miller's life ended tragically in 1944 when his plane crashed in the English Channel during World War II. A big-band festival, which attracts international performers, is held in his hometown.

Jerry Mathers, better known as Beaver Cleaver, was born in Sioux City.

On Television

Sioux City has turned out more than its share of television stars. Jerry Mathers, born in Sioux City in 1948, played young Theodore (Beaver) Cleaver on the popular series *Leave It to Beaver*. Fred Grandy, who played goofy Gopher on the original *Love Boat*, was also born in Sioux City. After his television career, he served Iowa's Sixth District in the U.S. House of Representatives from 1987 to 1995. Sharon Farrell, who played Flo Webster on the television soap opera *The Young and the Restless* calls Sioux City her home. Macdonald Carey, another daytime-drama star from Iowa, played Tom Horton on *Days of Our Lives*.

Long before comedians Jay Leno and David Letterman were hosting their late-night shows, Johnny Carson was on post-prime-time television. Born in Corning in 1925, Carson had a variety program before going on to *The Tonight Show Starring Johnny Carson*. From 1962 to 1992, he racked up more on-air hours than any other star in the history of television. The quick-thinking Carson was famous for his interviews and comedy skits.

Television journalist and longtime network news anchor Harry Reasoner was born in Dakota City in 1923. He was also a host on the weekly news television magazine *60 Minutes* before his death in 1991.

Richard Beymer, born in Avoca, played the character Benjamin Horne on *Twin Peaks*. Hope Emerson of Hawardan appeared in the detective show *Peter Gunn*, and the 1991 Graceland College graduate and Council Bluffs resident Davis Yost starred as Billy, the Blue Ranger, on the *Mighty Morphin Power Rangers*.

Comedian and *Tonight Show* host Johnny Carson was born in Corning.

Movie Stars

Old film comic Harry Langdon was born in Council Bluffs in 1884. He is still considered one of the top comics of the silent film era, rivaling such greats as Charlie Chaplin and Buster Keaton. Joan Freeman, also of Council Bluffs, played the female lead opposite rocker Elvis Presley in his film *Roustabout*. Then there is Terry Kiser, who starred in the title role of *Weekend at Bernie's*.

The rural countryside and hometown feel of Council Bluffs provided the backdrop for several films. Locals turned out to watch Barbara Stanwyck and her co-star Joel McCrea shoot the 1939 classic *Union Pacific*. Actor Sean Penn directed *The Indian Runner*, filmed in Council Bluffs in 1991.

Many other Iowa communities have native sons and daughters in films. One of the best known was the gravelly voiced, rough-and-rugged actor John Wayne, whose nickname was the Duke. Wayne was born Marion Morrison in the central Iowa town of Winterset in 1907. He changed his name to improve his chances in the movie business.

The modest four-room home where Wayne lived as a youngster has been restored and contains an impressive collection of John Wayne memorabilia. The display includes the eye patch he wore in the movie *True Grit*, his hat from *Rio Lobo,* and a prop suitcase used in *Stagecoach*, as well as hundreds of photographs and letters.

John Wayne was born in the town of Winterset.

The Charming Donna Reed

When she was active as a 4-H youngster, Donna Reed won a blue ribbon at the Iowa State Fair for her biscuits. But Reed did not want to spend her life on the family homestead in Denison. When she was sixteen, she hopped aboard a passenger train to Los Angeles to seek her fortune in films. Her small-town charm and pleasant personality earned her many significant film and television roles.

One of her most celebrated roles was as Jimmy Stewart's loyal wife, Mary, in the classic Christmas movie *It's a Wonderful Life*. She also won a 1953 Academy Award as best actress for her performance in *From Here to Eternity*. Reed's television show, *The Donna Reed Show*, which ran from 1958 to 1966, depicted the trials and tribulations of a family from that era. (Still from show at left, with Reed far left.)

Born in 1921, Reed died in 1986. The Donna Reed Festival for the Performing Arts is held each June in Denison. ■

A Music Man

Mason City native Meredith Willson wrote the popular Broadway musical (and later film) *The Music Man*. *The Music Man*, which used Iowa as its backdrop, told the story of a shady traveling salesman who peddled band uniforms to small towns. In his youth, Willson had been a flutist in the internationally known John Philip Sousa marching band. Perhaps that experience gave him ideas for *The Music Man*.

A noted musician and composer, Willson wrote the score for the 1940 film *The Great Dictator*, directed by the great Charlie Chaplin. In 1960, another popular Willson production was *The Unsinkable Molly Brown*, which was also made into a movie. Willson was born in 1902 and died in 1984. ■

Iowa's Literary Greats

Iowa has the highest literacy rate in the nation—more than 98 percent. Librarians and booksellers proudly say that Iowa residents read more books per capita than the people of any other state.

In the 1880s, Oil Coomes, a farmer from Wiota, wrote a series of inexpensive books called "dime-store novels," which sold thousands of copies. His action-packed tales such as *Hawkeye Harry*, *Tiger Tom,* and *The Texas Terror* excited and delighted his young readers.

Writer James Norman Hall, born in Colfax, Iowa, in 1887, wrote *Mutiny on the Bounty*, which was made into a film. He died in 1951. Fort Dodge native Thomas Heggen wrote about a naval officer in World War II in the best-selling novel, *Mister Roberts*, which was also made into a movie.

Mystery writer Virginia G. Rich was born in Sibley in 1914. She wrote *The Cooking School Murders*, *The Baked Bean Supper Murders*, and *The Nantucket Diet Murders*.

Mildred Wirt Benson, born in Ladora, published her first story

John Irving is among the famous graduates of the University of Iowa Writers' Workshop.

when she was only twelve years old and went on to write more than 130 books. She was the first of several authors who wrote the Nancy Drew mystery series. Girls enjoyed her portrayal of Nancy Drew as a strong female role model. In 1927, Mildred Wirt Benson, who wrote under at least ten different names, became the first woman to earn a master's degree in journalism from the University of Iowa.

Numerous writers from other states have studied at the University of Iowa Writers' Workshop in Iowa City since its founding in 1936. Among its graduates are the award-winning poets W. D. Snodgrass and Jorie Graham and best-selling novelists John Irving and Jane Smiley. Winner of the 1992 Pulitzer Prize for *A Thousand Acres*, Smiley earned several advanced degrees from the University of Iowa and taught at Iowa State University.

Iowa's Art World

The James and Meryl Hearst Center in Cedar Falls, Waterloo Museum of Art, Amana Arts Guild Gallery, and the MacNider Art Museum in Mason City are among the state's numerous arts centers and galleries. More than half a million people visit these attractions each year.

In the art world, sculptor Nellie Verne Walker was known as "the lady who lived on ladders." Barely 5 feet (1.5 m) tall, Walker used ladders to reach the top of her huge stone artworks. At age seventeen, her first piece, a bust of President Abraham Lincoln, was displayed at the 1893 Columbian Exposition. She was born in Red Oak in 1874 and died in 1973.

Painter Grant Wood established an art colony in 1932 in the town of Stone City. The house that he used as a background for his famous painting *American Gothic* still stands in Eldon. The building is on the National Register of Historic Places.

Contemporary painters, printmakers, and other artists born in Iowa include Kim Uchiyama, Dennis Kardon, Dennis Ashbaugh, Thomas Gormally, and Paula Elliott. Their use of vibrant color and treatment of hard-hitting themes have earned them international reputations.

A Festival of Iowa Folklife in 1996 marked the state's 150th anniversary. Artists and entertainers around the state took part in the birthday blowout. Audiences enjoyed listening to Decorah's Gordon MacMasters play the saw with a violin bow and the Mount Olive Baptist Church Choir sing spirituals in Sioux City. The Washington Municipal Band in concert added to the festivities.

The house shown in Grant Wood's *American Gothic* still stands in Eldon.

Sherman Place

The Hoyt Sherman Place in Des Moines was built in 1877 by a pioneer businessman and lawyer. During the Civil War, Sherman was an army paymaster. He was also the first postmaster of Des Moines and established the city's first bank, the waterworks, a public school, a college, and a life insurance company.

In 1907, after Sherman died, his house became the headquarters of the Des Moines Women's Club. The club constructed a theater with a domed ceiling attached to the house in 1923. The Sherman house now has a fine arts gallery with works by American and European artists as well as antiques. Recitals, concerts, and plays are shown regularly. The large brick building is on the National Register of Historic Places. ■

Sports

Iowa is crazy about sports. Stories about star athletes fill the sports pages of Iowa's twenty-five daily newspapers. Des Moines has its own sports radio station, KXLQ, featuring live coverage of games and talk shows.

The capital city is home to the Iowa Cubs, the AAA minor-league baseball team, and the Iowa Barnstormers Arena Football

Field of Dreams

Baseball lovers flock to the *Field of Dreams* movie site and ballpark near Dyersville every year. "If you build it, they will come" is the film's famous line. *Field of Dreams*, which stars Kevin Costner and was nominated for an Academy Award as best picture in 1989, is about a farmer who cuts a baseball diamond out of his cornfield. The ghosts of old-time ball players then emerge from the cornstalks to play for love of the game.

A Wall of Fame for Bob Feller

Bob Feller, a native of Van Meter, pitched for the Cleveland Indians from 1936 to 1956. Feller is a regular visitor at the Bob Feller Hometown Museum in Van Meter. The building opened in 1995, when Feller was seventy-seven years old. On an outside wall of the building, an interesting brickwork mural features the highlights of Feller's career, including his three no-hitters and his 1962 induction into the Baseball Hall of Fame. ■

club. The first season of the Des Moines Dragons basketball team in 1997 earned the team a playoff spot in the International Basketball Association League. Because the state has no major professional sports teams, college sports in Iowa attract die-hard fans.

Dan Gable of Waterloo, the state's wrestling legend, is billed as the "greatest pinner in college wrestling history." In his senior year of high school, Gable compiled a record of sixty-four wins and no losses. At Iowa State University, he was 116–1, losing the last match during the National Collegiate Athletic Association (NCAA) finals. He went on to win a gold medal in the 1972 Munich Olympics. As a wrestling coach at the University of Iowa, Gable led his squads to numerous victories. The Iowa Hawkeyes have won the NCAA Division I wrestling title nineteen times and captured the Big Ten Conference title for twenty-five straight years—a streak that Minnesota ended in 1999.

The University of Iowa is a powerhouse in many other sports too. A member of the Big Ten Conference, the Hawkeyes have long dominated basketball and football. Its football team won the national championship in 1958 and has gone to the Rose Bowl five times. The men's basketball team is also a perennial power. One of the most famous recent Hawkeye alums was B. J. Armstrong, who played from 1989 to 1995 alongside Michael Jordan in the Chicago Bulls' backcourt—and won three NBA championship rings as a result.

The Iowa State Cyclones also have some big-time college sports teams. They excel particularly at football, men's and women's basketball, and wrestling.

Recreation

Amateurs looking for fun in Iowa can find fishing, horseback riding, skydiving, skiing, hunting, soccer, hang gliding, horseshoe pitching, canoeing—and 265 golf courses. Thousands of cyclists take part in an annual bike marathon around Iowa.

Cycling is just one way Iowans stay busy.

Timeline

United States History

1607 The first permanent English settlement is established in North America at Jamestown.

1620 Pilgrims found Plymouth Colony, the second permanent English settlement.

1776 America declares its independence from Britain.

1783 The Treaty of Paris officially ends the Revolutionary War in America.

1787 The U.S. Constitution is written.

1803 The Louisiana Purchase almost doubles the size of the United States.

1812–15 The United States and Britain fight the War of 1812.

Iowa State History

1673 Father Jacques Marquette and Louis Jolliet canoe down the Mississippi River, arriving in what is now Iowa on June 25.

1680 René-Robert Cavelier, Sieur de La Salle, sends Michael Aco and Father Louis Hennepin to explore the Upper Mississippi River region.

1682 La Salle claims all the land drained by the Mississippi, including Iowa, for France.

1690 Nicholas Perrot teaches the Miami Indians how to mine lead.

1788 Julien Dubuque gets permission to mine lead in what is now Iowa.

1803 The United States acquires the Louisiana Purchase, which includes Iowa.

1805 Iowa becomes part of Louisiana Territory. Zebulon Pike visits Julien Dubuque's outpost and wants to mine more lead, beginning development of the area.

1812 Iowa becomes part of Missouri Territory.

1821 Iowa becomes unorganized land after state of Missouri is created.

United States History

The North and South fight **1861–65**
each other in the American Civil War.

The United States is **1917–18**
involved in World War I.

The stock market crashes, **1929**
plunging the United States into
the Great Depression.

The United States **1941–45**
fights in World War II.

The United States becomes a **1945**
charter member of the U.N.

The United States **1951–53**
fights in the Korean War.

The U.S. Congress enacts a series of **1964**
groundbreaking civil rights laws.

The United States **1964–73**
engages in the Vietnam War.

The United States and other **1991**
nations fight the brief
Persian Gulf War against Iraq.

Iowa State History

1832 The Sauk and Mesquakie are forced to
relinquish land in eastern Iowa as punishment for the Black Hawk War.

1834 Iowa becomes part of Michigan
Territory.

1836 Iowa becomes part of Wisconsin
Territory.

1838 Iowa Territory is established. It includes
parts of what are now Iowa, North and
South Dakota, and Minnesota.

1846 Iowa becomes the twenty-ninth state.

1867 The first railroad across Iowa is completed in Council Bluffs.

1920s Iowa farmers have trouble running
their farms due to low produce prices;
many farms are lost.

1960s–70s Iowa's districts are reapportioned.

1985 Iowa establishes a lottery.

1993 Much Iowa farmland and many cities
are devastated by the Great Flood.

Fast Facts

State capitol

Wild rose

Statehood date December 28, 1846, the 29th state

Origin of state name Indian word variously translated as "one who puts to sleep" or "beautiful land"

State capital Des Moines

State nickname The Hawkeye State

State motto "Our Liberties We Prize and Our Rights We Will Maintain"

State bird Eastern goldfinch

State flower Wild rose

State rock Geode

State tree Oak

State song "Song of Iowa"

Des Moines River

Des Moines

State fair	Mid-August in Des Moines
Total area; rank	56,276 sq. mi. (145,755 sq km); 26th
Land; rank	55,875 sq. mi. (144,716 sq km); 23rd
Water; rank	401 sq. mi. (1,039 sq km); 42nd
Inland water; **rank**	401 sq. mi. (1,039 sq km); 36th
Geographic center	Story, 5 miles (8 km) northeast of Ames
Latitude and longitude	Iowa is located approximately between 40° 36' and 43° 30' N and 89° 05' and 96° 31' W
Highest point	In Osceola County, 1,670 feet (509 m)
Lowest point	In Lee County, where the Mississippi and Des Moines Rivers merge, 480 feet (146 m)
Largest city	Des Moines
Number of counties	99
Population; rank	2,787,424 (1990 census); 30th
Density	50 persons per sq. mi. (19 per sq km)
Population distribution	61% urban, 39% rural

Ethnic distribution
(does not equal 100%)

White	96.63%
African-American	1.73%
Hispanic	1.18%
Asian and Pacific Islanders	0.92%
Other	0.46%
Native American	0.26%

Record high temperature	118°F (48°C) at Keokuk on July 20, 1934

Record low temperature	−47°F (−44°C) at Washta on January 12, 1912
Average July temperature	75°F (24°C)
Average January temperature	19°F (−7°C)
Average annual precipitation	32 inches (81 cm)

Natural Areas and Historic Sites

National Monuments

Effigy Mounds National Monument was named for the 200 mounds and 29 effigies of animals built by Eastern Woodland Indians from 500 B.C. to A.D. 1300. Outdoor lovers will also enjoy seeing the varied landscape, from tallgrass prairies to sparkling rivers.

National Historic Sites

Herbert Hoover National Historic Site is the birthplace and gravesite of the thirty-first U.S. president. Also on the grounds is the Hoover Presidential Library and Museum.

State Parks

Ledges State Park contains artifacts of early inhabitants dating back to 2,000 B.C. With its prairies, clearings, and woodlands, Ledges is popular with tourists who enjoy seeing the sights of the Des Moines River Valley.

Pilot Knob State Park and Recreation Area is a geologist's delight. This park includes a variety of wildlife; Dead Man's Lake, the state's only sphagnum bog—an area of spongy ground where moss turns into peat; and three types of rare pond lilies.

Malanaphy Springs State Preserve

Drake University Relays

Wapsipinicon State Park, one of the state's oldest parks, sits on the Wapsipinicon River. Its interesting landscape of moss-covered limestone and sandstone bluffs is popular with tourists and hikers.

Sports Teams

NCAA Teams (Division 1)

Drake University Bulldogs

Iowa State University Cyclones

University of Iowa Hawkeyes

University of Northern Iowa Panthers

Civic Center in Sioux City

Cultural Institutions

Libraries

The University of Iowa Libraries on the university's Des Moines campus include specialized libraries ranging from art to business. The main library has numerous collections, including the Iowa Women's Archives and the East Asian Collection.

The Herbert Hoover Presidential Library and Museum in West Branch has materials relating to the U.S. president, as well as the Roaring Twenties, Laura Ingalls Wilder, and the American Civil War.

The State Historical Society of Iowa Library, in Iowa City, offers information on the history of the state and of Iowan culture.

Museums

The Cedar Rapids Museum of Art holds the world's largest collections of paintings by Grant Wood, Marvin D. Cone, and Mauricio Lasansky. Its permanent collection includes more than 5,000 artworks.

University of Iowa

The Putnam Museum in Davenport is the oldest regional museum west of the Mississippi River. It is known for its outstanding Egyptian and animal artwork.

The Science Center of Iowa in Des Moines has numerous temporary exhibits, a planetarium, and permanent exhibits on kinetic sculpting, Foucault's pendulum, and images from the Hubble Space Telescope.

Performing Arts

Iowa has one major opera company, two symphony orchestras, and sixty-five theater groups.

Universities and Colleges

In the mid-1990s, Iowa had twenty public and forty-one private institutions of higher learning.

Annual Events

January–March

Okoboji Winter Games (late January)

St. Patrick's Day Celebration in Emmetsburg (second or third weekend in March)

April–June

Drake University Relays in Des Moines (April)

Tulip Festival in Orange City (May)

Tulip Time in Pella (May)

Dubuquefest in Dubuque (mid-May)

Grant Wood Art Festival in Stone City (second Sunday in June)

July–September

Riverboat Days in Clinton (early July)

River-Cade in Sioux City (mid-July)

Bix Beiderbecke Memorial Jazz Festival in Davenport (late July)

Nordic Fest in Decorah (late July)

Register's Annual Great Bicycle Ride across Iowa (late July)

Mesquakie Indian Powwow in Tama (August)

Iowa Championship Rodeo in Sidney (early August)

Iowa State Fair in Des Moines (August)

National Hot Air Balloon Classic in Indianola (early August)

National Hobo Convention in Britt (early August)

National Old Time Country Music and Festival in Avoca (August)

National Sprint Car Race Championship in Knoxville (mid-August)

Tri-State Rodeo in Fort Madison (early September)

Fort Atkinson Rendezvous (late September)

October–December

Covered Bridge Festival in Madison County (second weekend in October)

Forest Craft Festival in Van Buren County (mid-October)

Livestock shows at the National Dairy Cattle Congress in Waterloo (October)

Victorian Christmas in Albia (December)

Johnny Carson

Famous People

Adrian Constantine (Cap) Anson (1851–1922)	Baseball player and manager
Leon Bismarck (Bix) Beiderbecke (1903–1931)	Cornet player and composer
Black Hawk (1767–1838)	Sauk Indian cheif

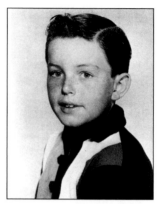

Jerry Mathers

Amelia Jenks Bloomer (1818–1894)	Social reformer
Norman Borlaug (1914–)	Crop geneticist and Nobel Prize winner
Johnny Carson (1925–)	Entertainer
Carrie Lane Chapman Catt (1859–1947)	Social reformer
William Frederick "Buffalo Bill" Cody (1846–1917)	Frontiersman and showman
Julien Dubuque (1762–1810)	Pioneer
Urban (Red) Faber (1888–1976)	Professional baseball player
Robert William Feller (1918–)	Baseball player
George Horace Gallup (1901–1984)	Statistician and public opinion analyst
Fred Grandy (1948–)	Actor and politician
James Norman Hall (1887–1951)	Author
Herbert Clark Hoover (1874–1964)	U.S. president
MacKinlay Kantor (1904–1977)	Author
Ann Landers (1918–)	Newspaper columnist
Cloris Leachman (1926–)	Actor
Jerry Mathers (1948–)	Actor
Glenn Miller (1904–1944)	Bandleader
Harry Reasoner (1923–1991)	Television journalist
Donna Reed (1921–1986)	Actor
Lillian Russell (1861–1922)	Singer and actor

John Wayne

William Ashley (Billy) Sunday (1862–1935)	Baseball player and evangelist
James Alfred Van Allen (1914–)	Astrophysicist
Abigail Van Buren (1918–)	Newspaper columnist
Henry Agard Wallace (1888–1965)	U.S. vice president
John Wayne (1907–1979)	Actor
Margaret Wilson (1882–1976)	Author
Grant Wood (1892–1942)	Artist

To Find Out More

History

- Fichter, George S., and Joe Boddy (illustrator). *First Steamboat Down the Mississippi*. Gretna, La.: Pelican, 1989.

- Fradin, Dennis Brindell. *Iowa*. Chicago: Children's Press, 1991.

- Ladoux, Rita C. *Iowa*. Minneapolis: Lerner, 1997.

- Lauber, Patricia. *Flood: Wrestling with the Mississippi*. Washington, D.C.: National Geographic Society, 1996.

- Thompson, Kathleen. *Iowa*. Austin, Tex.: Raintree/Steck Vaughn, 1996.

Fiction

- Harrison, Nick. *These Years of Promise: A Novel*. Kelowna, B.C.: Sunrise Books, 1988.

- Lawlor, Laurie, and Helen Cogancherry (illustrator). *Addie's Forever Friend*. Morton Grove, Ill.: Albert Whitman & Co., 1997.

Biography

- Clinton, Susan. *Herbert Hoover*. Chicago: Children's Press, 1988.

- Duggleby, John. *Artist in Overalls: The Life of Grant Wood*. San Francisco: Chronicle Books, 1996.

- Marvis, B. *Buffalo Bill Cody*. Broomall, Penn.: Chelsea House, 1999.

Websites

■ **The City of Des Moines**
http://www.ci.des-moines.ia.us/
For information on Iowa's capital

■ **IOWAccess**
http://www.state.ia.us
The official website for the Iowa state government

■ **The State Library of Iowa**
http://www.silo.lib.ia.us
For information on Iowa libraries and the state library's services

Addresses

■ **Iowa Department of Economic Development**
Division of Tourism
200 East Grand Avenue
Des Moines, IA 50309
For information on travel throughout Iowa

■ **Office of the Governor**
Iowa State Capitol
Des Moines, IA 50319
To contact Iowa's highest elected official

■ **Sioux City Art Center**
225 Nebraska Street
Sioux City, IA 51101
For information on this museum in Sioux City

Index

Page numbers in *italics* indicate illustrations.

Meet the Author

Martin Hintz was born and raised in New Hampton, Iowa, the county seat of Chickasaw County, in northeastern Iowa. His parents' families have lived in the Hawkeye State since the late 1880s. One of his grandfathers worked as a county sheriff, raised horses, and managed a road construction company and a silo manufacturing plant. His other grandfather was a farmer. Hintz was a student at St. Joseph's Grade School and New Hampton High. He attended Loras College in Dubuque for two years before graduating with a journalism degree from the College of St. Thomas in St. Paul, Minnesota.

To write this book, Martin Hintz did library and Internet research and conducted interviews with family members who still live in Iowa and other Iowans. He augmented it with his extensive personal knowledge of the state.

Hintz is the author of several books in the America the Beautiful and the Enchantment of the World series, published by Children's Press. He writes for numerous other publishers and produces the *Irish American Post*, a newsmagazine for Irish Americans that is distributed internationally.

Martin Hintz lives in River Hills, Wisconsin, with his wife, Pam Percy, a producer for Wisconsin Public Radio.

Photo Credits

Photographs ©:

Cameramann International, Ltd.: 65
Clint Farlinger: 7 top left, 44, 52, 55, 57, 58, 78 bottom, 110, 128 bottom, 129 top, 130
Corbis-Bettmann: 117, 133 (Scott Alonzo), 85 (Robert Maass), 38 (Reuters), 9 (Vince Streano), 66, 84 bottom, 92 top, 112, 119 (UPI), 16, 21, 27, 42, 84 top, 113, 116, 118 bottom, 121, 134 top
Courtesy of Governor's Office: 74, 76 left, 78 top
David Thoreson: 7 top right, 39, 51, 92 bottom, 100, 125
Dembinsky Photo Assoc.: 6 bottom, 56 top (Sharon Cummings)
Drake University Sports Information: 115, 131 top
Envision: 91 (Peter Johansky)
H. Armstrong Roberts, Inc.: cover, 73, 129 bottom (H. Abernathy), 6 top center, 69 (J. Blank), 34 (M. Gibson)
Iowa State University Library/University Archives: 41
Iowa Wesleyan College Archives: 30
John Deere North American Agricultural Marketing Center: 96
Liaison Agency, Inc.: 120 (Ulf Andersen), 79 (Terry Ashe), 111 (De Keerle/UK Press)

New England Stock Photo: 7 bottom, 114 (Dennis Clevenger), 104 (Karen J. Clevenger)
North Wind Picture Archives: 20, 23, 26
P. Michael Whye: 8, 61
Photri: 71, 109 (Lani Novak Howe), 107 (Bruce Leighty)
Ric Ergenbright: 83 (George Schwartz)
State Historical Society of Iowa: 14, 17, 22, 28, 33, 35, 37, 99, 101, 102, 106, 124
Stock Montage, Inc.: 98 (Tom Neiman), 19, 24, 25, 29, 32, 118 top, 134 bottom
Superstock, Inc.: 6 top left, 49, 59, 60, 89, 128 top
Tim Thompson: 62, 67, 76 right
Tom Till: 2, 11, 15, 45, 56 bottom, 87
Tony Stone Images: 40 (David Job), back cover (Ryan-Beyer), 88
Unicorn Stock Photos: 123 (Louie Bunde), 6 top right, 86 (Ed Harp), 36 (B. W. Hoffmann), 93 (Martha McBride), 7 top center, 12 (Norman A. Petersen II), 108 (Jerry Schnieders), 95, 122 (Jim Shippee), 70, 132 (Joe Sohm)
Viesti Collection, Inc.: 72 (Richard Cummins)
Visuals Unlimited: 63, 131 bottom (Louie Bunde), 48 (D. Cavagnaro), 53 (Cheryl A. Ertelt)
Maps by XNR Productions, Inc.